IN THE BEGINNING

LIFE LESSONS IN GENESIS

VIRGINIA WOOTEN
BARNES, ED.D.

WESTBOW
PRESS®
A DIVISION OF THOMAS NELSON
& ZONDERVAN

WestBow Press books may be ordered through booksellers or by contacting:

WestBow Press
A Division of Thomas Nelson & Zondervan
1663 Liberty Drive
Bloomington, IN 47403
www.westbowpress.com
844-714-3454

ISBN: 979-8-3850-3133-7 (sc)
ISBN: 979-8-3850-3135-1 (hc)
ISBN: 979-8-3850-3134-4 (e)

Library of Congress Control Number: 2024917260

Print information available on the last page.

WestBow Press rev. date: 09/26/2024

SPECIAL THANKS

I thank the dear ones in my Bible studies who suggested that I write this book (you know who you are). I give special thanks to my husband, children and grandchildren for their encouragement and delight in these Genesis stories. Lord, I thank you for their love, ideas and support.

This book was conceived inside the heart and mind of God. I give thanks for the revelations in each Genesis chapter. These stories of God's people share profound truths that are life lessons for today. May these colorful stories inspire you.

TABLE OF CONTENTS

THE ANCIENT WORLD OF THE BIBLE

HELPFUL HINTS FOR UNDERSTANDING

THE ANCIENT WORLD
OF THE BIBLE
HELPFUL HINTS FOR
UNDERSTANDING

Introduction: By reading, studying and discussing Genesis, you will be stepping into an *ancient world*, many thousands of years before our modern world. Some issues in the chapters could seem problematic at first glance. Remind yourself that you are *unpacking God's life lessons*, rather than challenging the science or accuracy of the details. *Here are some hints for helpful understanding and questions you might wish to explore on your own.*

Science of Creation: Presently, scientists still disagree on when the world came into being and how large the universe really is. The "Big Bang" era is now being questioned and debated as to when the first of the planets and stars were formed, as scientists interpret the latest evidence from the James Webb Space Telescope. *Good questions for discussion are: Are the Creation Story and the Flood Story true and accurate? How many Flood and Creation stories are found in ancient times? Are they similar?*

Population Growth: There is no limit to how far in the past we humans came into being. Scientists often disagree on how much of the Ancient World was populated and when people began spreading out of Africa. All of this speculation naturally changes as scientists discover more evidence through advanced exploration and archaeological finds. *Good questions to ask are: How did the population grow, where did people live, who did they marry, how long did they live? Is the story of Babel true? How did all the different peoples of the world come into being?*

Geography, Cities, Lands: The stories of Genesis take place around the Fertile Crescent, the Tigris and Euphrates Rivers, The Great Sea (Mediterranean Sea), the lands of Egypt, Canaan and the Philistines, and in cities of Ur, Shechem, Gaza, Gerar, Bethel, Haran, Hebron, Sodom and Gomorrah, Beersheba, Salem and more . You will read of tribes of the Semites, Hittites, Canaanites, Edomites, Ishmaelites and others as tribal families grew and merged together. Farther away from the Fertile Crescent the weather was dry, hot, windy and famine was experienced regularly. The digging of good wells was a precious commodity and often problematic regarding ownership. *Good questions to ask are: What crops were the best to grow? Did they grow grapes for wine? How did they cook their food? How difficult was it to dig a proper water well?*

Name and Character of God: The name for God changes throughout Genesis chapters. References to the Almighty were the names God, El or Elohim, LORD, or LORD God and are used throughout Genesis. Depending on what scribe recorded the stories or the time in which it was recorded, the name for God changes throughout the different chapters. You may note in my writings that I chose to use the name of God given in the specific scripture story under discussion. The characteristics of the Holy One change over time as the people grasp and explain the concept. Idol worship was common in many geographical areas. The worship of fertility gods was important to women, and it was not uncommon for them to worship both God as well as idols. The Patriarch's God expressed feelings, presence, personality, and spoke directly to individuals. Angels were described to accompany the

LORD GOD. This could not be said for the idols. *Good questions to ask are: How did people share their faith? What is the evolution of public worship?*

Social Norms: Women's opinions and roles in society were limited, and it is fairly easy to observe in the Genesis stories that manipulation was used to encourage the male partner to cooperate. Women had the societal expectation to bring life into the world. Bearing children and caring for the home was the most important aspect of the female role. Women were ostracized or blamed when they were unable to get pregnant, a common theme in Genesis. Often women referred to God as the powerful one who was responsible for closing or opening their womb. *Good questions to ask are: Why was it okay to have concubines to help produce more children for the wife? How early or late of age could women have children? How were women treated who never got pregnant?*

Lifestyle: The lands of the Fertile Crescent and areas bordering it were good for crops, livestock grazing, population growth, and communication. Around the Mediterranean travel was increasing and sharing of domestic production was offering an improved lifestyle. Wealth was determined or defined by number of livestock, crops, servants and family size. The patriarchs and their families were known to settle in various areas where the land and water would produce increased supply. Many were nomadic, setting up tents, then moving on when they needed more room or experienced disruption in the land such as famine, wars or conflict over resources. *Good questions to ask are: Were the patriarchs considered wealthy? Was it legal to have many servants and maid servants? When did the patriarchs settle into cities and no longer were nomadic?*

Life, Birth and Death: Childbirth was dangerous and difficult for many women, and many died during the process. Children were a valuable resource and honor was given to women who had many, especially male children. Unscientific magic cures were sometimes adopted to help cause pregnancy; and were used for both animal and human births. The lifespan in Genesis was incredibly generous, with people living many hundreds of years. That long life span was helpful in populating the earth. *Good questions to ask are: How early did girls marry and start having children? Did women have a choice in the person they married?*

Reading Recommendations: As you read each of the chapters of Genesis, enjoy the words themselves and picture in your mind what the story looks or feels like to you. I suggest reading the scripture listed first and focusing on the key verse. Next, read the story I wrote for you. *Each of these stories is meant as a **life lesson**. You might ask what God's message is for you in every story.* Enjoy the feeling you have at the moment. Then pray the prayer.

NOTES:

IN THE BEGINNING

NEW BEGINNINGS

SCRIPTURE: *Genesis 1:1-25*

KEY VERSE: *Genesis 1: 1-2*

God's creation was a time of newness and promise. It was a blank slate. Our Creator's new world began with an empty, dark, and formless heaven and earth. Then God's Spirit acted and began to "hover" over the waters. To "hover" means to begin to do something.

Now, my favorite "Deep South" phrase for hover is *"fixin' to"*, meaning an announcement of preparation for action of some sort. Growing up in the southern United States we loved all types of unique phrases, yet this one phrase was POWERFUL! The reason? It was a statement made to others. It was when you would announce WHAT you were about to DO! For example, my mother might say *"I'm fixin' to"* go make dinner." That meant you could expect her to begin activity in the kitchen.

That's what God's beginnings were all about. You see, God was "*fixin' to*" create something. He was at the very beginnings of creating our world and He was making that announcement. According to the author of Genesis, God was speaking the world into existence. The Genesis account also tells us that God had high standards as He hovered over the waters. Following each creation activity, God declared that it was *good*. An orderly God created day and night/ sky/ land and sea/ sun, moon and stars/ creatures for land, water, and sky/ and lastly man and woman. When God completed His sixth and final activity, God added the adverb "*very*" to His statement, making all creation activities *very good*. I offer the opinion that God was pretty proud of his handiwork!

When you are contemplating changes in your own life, you are taking action to create something new, hovering over what kind of new life you hope for or desire. By the way, take a tip from our Creator and adopt an orderly plan of management and evaluation. Bottom line: whatever you are "*fixin'*" to do, may it be *VERY GOOD!*

PRAYER:
Dear God, thank you for your creation and for new beginnings. Amen.

NOTES:

U R HOLY

SCRIPTURE: *Genesis 1:26-31*

KEY VERSE: *Genesis 1:26-27*

God created us in God's own likeness. What an incredible potential we have to be in the likeness of God! God is a holy, righteous, loving, and compassionate thinker and creator. *Can we really be like God?* How can we feel, think and act like God? Without God in our heart it is an impossibility. So how do we keep the characteristics of God in our heart and mind? It takes a loving God, patience, dedication, scripture, study, and prayer continuously. In spite of all this planning and work, sometimes we still fall short of our goal.

As our children were growing up, we tried to teach them to behave in a Godly way because that is God's standard. That didn't mean that they were better than anyone else, but it was God's desire. *"Remember, you are Holy!"* was the mantra, which they probably grew weary of hearing. One day, I realized what a poor role model I was. Here's my short story. I was running around like a mad woman, getting packed, trying to catch a flight and run an important errand. And it was raining! Short fused and insensitive to everyone in the family, I left a wake of hurt feelings behind. My errand finished, I jumped in the car, and noticed a note under my windshield wipers. Furious at the annoyance, I grabbed the paper, threw it inside on the front seat and wheeled out of the parking lot to a red light. At that moment, the note fell over, and I recognized the handwriting. It was my youngest daughter's. While waiting for the green light, I read her words: *"Mom, Remember, UR HOLY."* "Forgive me, Lord, I prayed." And later made the same request to my family. This was a needed reminder. *I was God's creation meant to be like my Creator. Full of holiness, love, and compassion. I needed to be better at this.*

Try not to get discouraged when you are trying to do your best to be the holy person God desires for you. Our God created YOU for great and wonderful plans. And He is patient and loving.

PRAYER

Lord, live in my heart and mind. Guide me to be more like you and to treat others as you would want me to. Amen

NOTES:

GOD RESTS

Scripture: Genesis 2: 1-3

Key Verse: Genesis 2:3

Do you take naps? Some people take "power naps". These are just short 20–30-minute naps, maybe on a couch or chair in the office or home. Just that short naptime could provide lots of energy for the rest of the workday. Clear eyed and full of "get up and go" people could perform better. I never could get that concept right. If I went to sleep during the day, I was down and out for at least two hours, then I felt "hung over" the rest of the day. In our culture we tend to work all day and sometimes into the evening. With technology we carry our work with us, always checking for the latest call, text or email we must answer.

So, is there a better plan? *Think so!* And God was

the first user of His plan which later became one of the Ten Commandments: a call to remember the Sabbath and keep it holy. The "Sabbath" actually means rest. Our Creator knew our bodies, minds and souls needed rest in order to perform well and live a well-balanced life. If God needed rest, we certainly do! Sabbath is a time to focus on God's blessings and grace. It's time to enjoy family and friends. It's time to lay aside worries, our to-do lists and say aloud, "I am finished with my work demands." It's a time to worship God at home, in nature, at a church or in a synagogue, or temple. Remember, God rested because God had *finished* creation.

A friend of mine has a technique she uses to prepare for the Sabbath, and it isn't even a spiritual activity. Before leaving her workplace, she places her " to do list" in her desk drawer, closes the drawer, puts her hands over the drawer and speaks aloud these words: "Stay." She says that the activity causes her to leave work behind and focus on her Sabbath moments.

PRAYER:

Dear God, I want to have Sabbath moments with you every day, not just on a Saturday or Sunday. My desire is to have a holy, restful time daily in your presence. It will be my power nap with you. Amen

NOTES

GARDEN OF EDEN

SCRIPTURE: *Genesis 2:8-25*
KEY VERSES: *Genesis 2:8-9*

My husband and I have experienced some of the most beautiful gardens in our international travels. Our top three favorites were: Claude Monet's Garden in Giverny, France; Singapore's Garden by the Bay; and the Garden of Villandry in Loire, France. All were absolutely magnificent, yet very different from one another. While these were lovely gardens, I think that the Garden of Eden, natural architect God, must have been out of this world!

The Pishon, Gihon, and the Tigris and Euphrates, which we identify today, watered God's gardens. Genesis describes it as a rich, lush, and beautiful paradise, with cool winds and good smelling aromas. Trees bearing fruits and nuts to eat were abundant.

The LORD GOD told Adam to take care of it and offered that he could eat from any tree in the garden with one exception. He warned Adam that he would die if he ate from the tree that had the knowledge of good and evil. It was in the middle of the garden.

It was here, in this beautiful world, that God formed and placed birds, and other animal creatures and asked Adam to name them. Then, best of all, the LORD GOD gave Adam a wife, Eve. Made from Adam's rib bone, the first woman and mother of mankind, emerged as a compliment for Adam. He was now whole, united with his woman. Eve was to be his companion, partner, help mate, his love, his precious wife. It was to be a monogamous union, ordained by the Creator of all things. What a beautiful paradise this was for Adam and Eve. Their gift from God, the Creator, to enjoy together.

We, too, can enjoy the beauty of our world every day, in every season. Take time to relish the land, skies, vegetation, food, animals and most importantly, relish those you love and thank them for their meaning in your life. Let us care for all of our blessings from God.

PRAYER:

Creator God, thank you for the beauty you have given us. Help us to be good stewards of this world. May our relationships provide a wholeness of life, and a partnership to make a family and improve the world. Amen

NOTES:

THE FALL

SCRIPTURE: *Genesis 3: 1-7*

KEY VERSE: *Genesis 3:6*

Are you easily persuaded to do something? Do you excel as a persuasive person? Some people can be labelled "manipulative" when they desire something for themselves. In this ancient Mediterranean culture, the female voice was often deemed unimportant so being a savvy persuader could sometimes help a woman get what she wants. *Eve set the standard in Genesis for being a persuasive woman.*

Throughout history, Eve has taken the hit for getting the first couple in trouble with God. She was persuaded by the serpent to do what God had warned her husband Adam NOT to do. God warned Adam that he could eat from any tree in the garden, but he would die if he ate from the tree that had knowledge of good and evil. Even though God told Adam when he was by himself, Adam would have informed Eve of that danger. Was Eve confused or wavering about what Adam may have told her? Attempting to be savvy and appear informed, Eve offered her tree knowledge to the inquiring serpent. The serpent asked: (my words) *Just to be clear, you can't eat from any tree in the garden?* Eve replied: *(my words) Just the tree in the middle of the garden, and if we eat it or even touch it, we'll die.*" Eve was showing off to the serpent and clearly embellished the facts. It was the eating of the fruit that would cause trouble, NOT the touching of the fruit. Nevertheless, Eve must have believed the fruit would be tasty and was worth the risk. Eve ate the fruit and gave some to Adam who also ate it. Had he forgotten what God had said? Could he have refused and reminded Eve what God's warning was? Eve must have been very persuasive, as was the serpent. And the outcome? Their eyes were opened. Stay tuned.

In our lives we sometimes run across people who persuade us to engage in activities we have no business getting involved in. Trying to be savvy and a "know it all" can get us in trouble. In the process of trying to look smart, we often fall for the invitation to "eat of the forbidden fruit."

PRAYER:
Dear Lord, thank you for the provisions you have given us. All that we have is from you and we are grateful. Help us to obey you and understand your will. Amen

NOTES:

"WHERE ARE YOU?"

SCRIPTURE: *Genesis 3: 7- 24*
KEY VERSE: *Genesis 3: 8-9*

Hide and seek is a fun game. "I'll count to ten, you hide, and I'll come find you," we say. Children can find interesting places to hide like a closet, pantry, or a box. I know a little boy who liked to hide in the dirty clothes hamper, but his sisters knew his plan and could always find him.

God knows our ways, just as God knew what the first couple had done. He knew where to find them. Observing their nakedness for the first time, Adam and Eve hid among the trees. God called to Adam, asking where he was hiding. Then, God asked Eve, what mess have you created? God already knew the answers.

Standing face to face with God, each pointed

blaming fingers away from themselves. Adam blamed Eve and Eve blamed the serpent. Adam also seemed to blame God. After all, God had given Eve to him, and she was the problem! The scripture is silent if Adam and Eve showed any signs of remorse or a plea for forgiveness. Could their lack of repentance have added to God's displeasure with them? Due to disobedience, God tossed the first couple out of Eden into a life of hard work. The serpent was cursed, Eve got pain in childbearing, and Adam had to work hard to toil the ground. The" paradise lost" story is complicated, yet we can recognize the consequences of disobedience.

Where are we? Where did we go wrong? What is the next step? Can we find God in the midst of our own waywardness? The answer is YES! Asking God and others for forgiveness results in restoration of the relationship. Yet, we never forget the results of the hurt and the memory. We desire a "do over" and want to be a better person. Adam and Eve had to leave their beautiful life God had provided. That life was over. God was firm. Yet, God still loved them and as they left Eden God made clothes for them and covered their nakedness. God can cover our own shame and our sins. We just have to believe and repent.

PRAYER:
Holy One, thank you for caring to protect us, even when we have disobeyed you. You are our father who desires our safety and life. Forgive our sins and abide with us. Amen.

NOTES:

FAMILY HISTORY

MY BROTHER'S KEEPER

SCRIPTURE: Genesis 4: 1-16

KEY VERSE: Genesis 4:8-9

Brother's keeper? Was that Cain's job? He didn't think so. Cain, son of Adam and Eve, was filled with jealousy and rage and committed a preplanned heinous crime: the murder of his own brother, Abel. Cain was angry because God had shown favor on brother Abel's offering, but not on his own. God warned Cain that he needed to get control of his anger. Unable to do so, Cain killed Abel. God confronted Cain, asked him to explain and received a sarcastic reply: (my words) "not my brother's keeper!" As a consequence God cursed Cain's land and made him to wander, be restless and no longer know God's presence. That was more than Cain could bear.

Cain's banishment was similar to that of his parents, Adam and Eve. God confronted the first couple asking questions he already knew the answer to. God's punishment for them was banishment from Eden and a hard life. As they left Eden, God provided clothing to cover their nakedness. Cain was banished from God's presence, but God provided a special mark on Cain to protect and prevent him from being harmed. Cain settled in the land of Nod, east of Eden, forever estranged from God.

Being our "brother's keeper" is a biblical concept most people, even children, can know the meaning. Years ago, our four children knew that when our house was for sale and being shown by a realtor, they needed to play outside. That meant the older two watched out for the younger two. One time the older two headed outside saying, "Don't worry, we'll be our brother and sister's keepers!! I was confident they would do a wonderful job!

Our world needs us to be our brothers' and sisters' keeper. Around the globe people are suffering from war, famine, displacement, and death of loved ones. Sometimes we allow our different beliefs to prevent us from helping others. Our angry disagreements and actions never work. We may be very different from others but love always works. Let us do our part.

PRAYER: Thank you, God, for continuing to love and care for us, even when we disappoint you. Guide me to walk in your ways. May we feel a call to care for others who need our help. Amen

NOTES:

THE FAMILY OF CAIN

SCRIPTURE: Genesis 4:17-24

KEY VERSE: Genesis 4:17

Last we read, Cain was distraught, restless, and wandering. God protected him with a mark, so no one would kill him. Living away from the Lord meant Cain was on his own. Cain built a city, settled, married, and began a family. In Genesis chapter four, seven generations are identified from the first family. Cain had Enoch, father of Irad, who had Mehujael, father of Methushael, who had Lamech.

Scripture is silent on details of the generations until we reach Lamech, the seventh generation. Something was eroding the family line. Could it be the impact of the curse that God placed on Cain? Could Lamech have had something to prove? We read that Lamech married two women, Adah, and

Zillah, indicating evidence of polygamy. Adah had Jabal; who lived in tents and raised livestock. Jubal, his brother became a musician and played the harp and flute. Zillah had Tubal-Cain, who worked with bronze and iron. His sister was Naamah.

God's plan in Eden was one husband, one wife. Lamech is described as a haughty man who would do things his own way. This pride can be observed in Lamech's announcement to his two wives that he had killed a man to avenge Cain's murder of Abel. Taking another person's life would not change the curse of Cain on their family.

It is difficult in life to outrun a negative reputation of someone in your family. Never being able to escape that unfair label can be heartbreaking. Lamech had something to prove, yet he tried to solve it himself.

If this is happening in your life or the life of someone you know, God's Spirit can heal. Pray for God to help a family's reputation, to purify their hearts and heal family relationships. We can walk with God, with our heads held high and love in our hearts.

PRAYER: Dear God, thank you for your power and grace. I place my sorrow, my history, my family in your loving hands. Make us whole again, loving one another and walking with you always. Amen

NOTES:

THE FAMILY OF SETH

SCRIPTURE: *Genesis 5*

KEY VERSE: *Genesis 5: 3-5*

Family history can provide evidence of longevity. We can predict the length of our lives based on how long our great, great, grandparents and own parents lived. We can compare our DNA with family health issues, illnesses, maladies, or circumstances such as accidents or war. Today, the average anticipated age at death is higher due to good medical care, pharmaceuticals, and nutrition. Even having friendships and spouses raise the bar! My mother-in-law lived to 97, so I expect my husband, who is in good health, to be with me a long time!

However, nothing can beat the longevity of the first families from Adam to Noah. Whether the ages mentioned in *Genesis 5* are literal or symbolic is a continued debate. Look at these lifespans of the family of Seth. Seth the father of Enosh lived 912 years; Enosh father of Kenan lived 905 years; Kenan father of Mahalalel lived 910 years; Mahalalel father of Jared lived 895 years; Jared father of Enoch lived 962 years; Enoch father of Methuselah lived 365 years; Methuselah father of Lamech lived 969 years; Lamech father of Noah lived 777 years; Noah, father of Shem, Ham and Japheth lived 950 years. Seems our Creator truly was serious about populating the earth. By providing long lives many descendants were born.

It's pretty clear that God's plan was going along just fine, despite a few hiccups, and the world was getting populated quickly due to the longevity of the first families. However, something caused God to act drastically. Stay tuned for the wickedness to increase among God's humanity.

Our globe today is filled to the brink with populations in all nations. Each nation has its own issues to serve its people. We can share in solving the problems of health, hunger, climate, medicine and education. Are you called to be a hero for the people of our world?

PRAYER: Dear God, thank you for your creation plan. Your power to create and then populate the world is beyond our imagination. We observe your beauty in all you create. Help us to serve one another and keep caring for our world. Amen.

NOTES:

THE FLOOD

SCRIPTURE: *Genesis 6: 1-22*
KEY VERSE: *Genesis 6:6-7*

Have you ever been so aggravated with someone that you were just ready to quit? Did you ever work so diligently on something that was so perfect, and then someone came along and destroyed it? As a lame example, I recall my high school science project I just knew could win a prize. When loading it into my parents' car, my high school helpers dropped it, and it broke to pieces! I desperately wanted a "do over."

God was divinely frustrated and sorrowful about his creation of humankind. He wanted a "do-over." In Genesis 6:1-7 we read that the humans of the world were making a mess of things. The population was increasing, and godly sons were marrying sinful women. Wickedness and violence were everywhere.

There is a mysterious reference to the Nephilim, large strong sinful men, who were doing great harm. It seemed to God that mankind only had evil thoughts all the time. God knew that limiting the longevity of humans was a timely act. There were just too many people doing sinful things.

God decided to destroy the people by flood, but he also had a backup plan to save a few righteous humans. God noticed Noah, who was righteous and so God saved Noah and his family. You know the story. God told Noah to build an ark and gave him the blueprints, a list of people to include, and every kind of animal, and food to put inside. God was serious. And Noah did what God said. The outcome? When the floods came, others were destroyed, but Noah's family was safe from the waters that flooded the earth for 150 days.

God has the power to provide and the power to discipline. He has the power to give and the power to take away. Is it possible that the Almighty sees evil everywhere in the world today? May we stay faithful to God, follow His ways and seek forgiveness.

PRAYER: Dear God, thank you for being our safe haven. You rescue us from harm. We are filled with wrongdoing, yet you love us. Noah's ark is a sign of your grace. Amen.

NOTES:

RAINBOW COVENANT

SCRIPTURE: *Genesis 7 -9*

KEY VERSES: *Genesis 9: 11,13*

It's raining hard today as I am writing from my home. The waters are gushing from the hills to our creek behind the house. It has not stopped all day. Flood warnings are on the news. I wonder how destructive the water will be.

I think of Noah who, faithful to God, built the ark, and was saved from the flood that God had sent to destroy a sinful world. God chose to save Noah's family and a selection of all the animals on the earth. It took 150 plus days before the ark landed on the Ararat mountains. Responses from a raven and dove gave Noah an idea of the level of the flood waters. He was looking for dry land. When Noah and his family came out of the ark, he built an altar to the LORD.

Noah and his family were faithful and when dry land had appeared they received a promise and covenant with God. The rainbow was a sign of the covenant that God would never create a flood to destroy the earth.

The Almighty is a God of consequences, yet His grace is perfectly given to those who are faithful to Him. Noah was the first biblical character to receive a covenant with God and he was saved from the flood in order to do what God intended for the earth. God wanted Noah and his family to grow and populate the earth, and to care for the living things of the earth. That is God's call for us today. We share in that responsibility.

My local rainstorm has ceased, and the sun has come out. The fallen raindrops now seem to sparkle on each leaf of the trees, bushes, and the grass. I smile at the wonder. It reminds me of God's love for us. I am grateful for Noah, his family, and God's promise to each of us through the Noahic covenant. Today, the rainbow remains as a reminder of God's grace.

How can we share the concept of God's grace? In what ways can we celebrate the world and humankind by caring for it and others? The responsibility is now our own.

PRAYER: God, thank you for the beauty of creation and your grace and love. May we be responsible for caring for creation and loving others. Amen

NOTES:

TOO MUCH WINE?

SCRIPTURE: *Genesis 9: 18-29*
KEY VERSE: *Genesis 9:22*

   Privacy and respect are two important characteristics when dealing with others. Gossiping about someone does not include either characteristic. By the time gossip is retold to many people it is blown out of proportion. It can be hurtful and bewildering when it circles back to the person being gossiped about. Ever been the brunt of gossip? Was it hard to ever again trust the person who started the rumor mill? Families can have issues like that when members talk about the other behind their back. Such was the case with Noah, who drank too much wine and unfortunately exposed himself unaware to any peeping Tom.

   It appears that Noah planted a vineyard after

settling in from the flood. He must have been successful at making tasty wine, for in this story he drank more than necessary, and he became drunk. Asleep in the middle of the day, he forgot to cover himself and exposed his manly parts to whomever peeked inside the tent. Son Ham not only peeked but shared with his two brothers what he saw. Scripture is silent on what he said, but I imagine he was poking fun at his dad and showing a lack of respect. After Ham's description, his brothers Shem and Japeth respectfully covered Noah by walking backwards into his tent, so as not to glance at his body. When Noah discovered the incident, he was furious with Ham and cursed Ham's son, Canaan. In ancient times curses were a way of predicting negative future outcomes, while blessings were positive future outcomes.

Why Canaan and not Ham, you ask? Ever heard the expression *like father, like son*? Noah predicted that Canaan would turn out to be like his dad. Parents often pass down their behavioral characteristics to their children, who copy them, sometimes to the extreme. Noah forecast what would happen with Canaan in the future. And sure enough, the Canaanite Tribe indeed had conflict with God's chosen patriarchal families.

Turns out we are examples to our children. In what ways do we need to clean up our own act? Worth pondering.

PRAYER:
Dear God, may I remember to be respectful of others and show love and concern to my friends and family. Amen

NOTES:

THE TABLE OF
NATIONS

SCRIPTURE: Genesis 10
KEY VERSE: Genesis 10:1

Do you keep track of your ancestors and enjoy the discoveries of genealogical studies? Seems that was important to the ancients. I find the accounts in Genesis to be mind boggling and exceptional because of the times in which they were recorded. These accounts help us answer the question often asked: *"where did all the different people come from to populate the world? "* We are blessed to have ancient tribal leaders, scribes, and family historians who were diligent in keeping both oral and written records, many of which are found on stone slabs, clay tablets, parchment, and animal skins. Inevitably, they do not include everyone, yet offer an array of names we can associate with ancient peoples, cities, and nations.

The Table of Nations gives accounts of the tribes of the sons and grandsons of Noah: Japheth, Ham, and Shem. *Approximately 70 nations came from the three brothers.* The descendants are mentioned as nations and peoples who spread out north and west from Palestine, forming their own language. Japheth's descendants (Gomer, Magog, Meshech and Togarmah) and Ham's descendants (Cush, Put) are prophesied in Ezekial 38-39 as nations to war against Israel. Gomer's sons, Ashkenaz, and Tarshish, are familiar names in the Hebrew Bible. Ham's son Cush was the father of Nimrod, a mighty warrior involved in the Tower of Babel. Canaan, also son of Cush, was father of the Hittites, Jebusites (inhabitants of Jerusalem during King David's conquest), Amorites and Hivites. *Shem's descendants are the Semites, God's chosen line of Abraham*

The upcoming story of the Tower of Babel in Genesis 11 nestles neatly with the facts in the Table of Nations, as it illustrates how and why the post flood peoples scattered to form new nations in their known world. *The Almighty had a plan all along! We are a result of that plan.*

How does our past influence our future decisions? How can we celebrate the differences between the people in the nations of the world? What role do we have?

PRAYER: *Thank you, God, for your creation, for all the peoples of the ancient world and your divine plan to choose the line to the Abrahamic Covenant. Amen*

NOTES:

BABEL, BABY TALK?

SCRIPTURE: Genesis 11:1-8
KEY VERSE: Genesis 11: 4

You just got to love little babies, and the way they just go on babbling, trying so hard to mimic our spoken language. They are adorable as they "practice talk." I believe somehow, they know what they are saying! Often, it is only the parents who can translate. Today, we use the term "babbling" without realizing that it may have originated in this biblical story of the Tower of Babel. Furthermore, there is a probability that the city of Babylon itself resides within the same geographic area as Shinar, where this story takes place.

The LORD had a conundrum with the arrogant people of Shinar. They were excessively focused on building a ziggurat or a stairway to the heavens. They wanted to build it all the way to reach the LORD. It was their ego in charge as they wanted others to see their importance. Shinar apparently wanted to have the biggest and best! That arrogance didn't sit well with the LORD and He had to figure out a way to stop them. So, the LORD confused their language causing them not to be able to work together. They stopped building and things were in chaos. As a result of the confusion, people left the area and settled away from the city into other geographic parts of the land. This is an interesting story to explain how many other nations, cultures and languages were formed.

Another good lesson from the story is this: Confusion in our life can cause us to misunderstand what God wants for us. Our ego may be influenced by others, or we just fail to listen to God's prompts in our minds and hearts. In what ways can we organize our thoughts to focus on what is most important in our lives? God desires our attention and worship every day. *A possible answer may be to modify our daily activities or events and ask the big question "what is most important in my life?" Something to think about.*

PRAYER: God, help us to know your desires for us and to have the strength to move forward. I want to know your will and to always follow you. Amen

NOTES

NOAH TO ABRAM

SCRIPTURE: Genesis 11: 10-32
KEY VERSE: Genesis 11: 27

Today I am hanging old family photos on a wall in my study. These photos indicate how our DNA runs through generations of our family. Hair styles, clothing, and photo processing are different from today. Nevertheless, it's clear from our likenesses that we are all one family.

The generations of Abram's family are made clear for us in Genesis 11. Beginning with the family of Noah, God chose the DNA line of Noah's son Shem to build *a genealogy to Abram!* This is an incredible Biblical legacy for us.

If this were today's digital genealogical research, Abram and Sarai might have proudly hung photos on their walls (maybe tents ?) of relatives named Noah,

Shem, Arphaxad, Shelah, Eber, Peleg, Reu, Serug, Nahor and Terah, Abram's father. Their relatives probably had characteristics indicating they were all one family. Noah's family genealogy takes my breath away. *Abram came from the DNA of Noah*, the most righteous man whose family was chosen to survive the flood. Noah's DNA was passed on through the generations. Our Creator had Abram in mind when he saved Noah's family. God knew that Abram would be righteous and be chosen to participate in God's covenant!

God has a legacy and plans for us before we are conceived. With gratitude and thanksgiving, I see God's perfect plan in photos that are now hanging on my study wall. And your legacy? What has God called you to become in your own life? Are you called to be a minister or a church deacon? Maybe a missionary in Africa or elsewhere? Perhaps you are called to build a large family who loves God or a family farm who breeds cattle and raises crops? Maybe you are a writer, singer, speaker, teacher, physician, professor, painter, reporter, novelist or news anchor or producer. Whatever it is, God has planned and prepared a way for you, just as He did for Noah, Shem, Abram and their families. We know this because we are reading their stories. And those are also our stories.

PRAYER: Almighty One, thank you for your goodness, faithfulness, and love. Thank you for the plans you orchestrate in our world, family, and our lives. Amen.

NOTES:

ABRAHAM

THE CALL

SCRIPTURE: *Genesis 12: 1-4*

SCRIPTURE VERSE: *Genesis 12: 4*

When I was young my grandma (aka "Big Mama") would answer the phone this way: "*Who is it?*" This was the 1950's, way before caller ID or cell phones, so she wanted to know "who's calling" immediately. I wonder, did Abram want to ask, "Who is it?" when God came calling?

We don't know what Abram THOUGHT or SAID, we only know what he DID. He acted immediately and left his home in Haran because the LORD told him to. He was faithful and obedient. Now, it's important to note that the LORD didn't give Abram a choice. He didn't say "*Hey, Abram, how would you like to leave Haran, and all your friends and family? I got something to show you."* Instead, the LORD said, "LEAVE AND GO."

Now, I imagine that the enticement was when the LORD described what he had planned for Abram: *great nation, great name, be a blessing, be blessed, have curse protection and entire people of the earth be blessed.* That was the LORD's offer, and it was amazing! However, notice that the LORD didn't offer any specifics such as the HOW he was going do all the things He promised. What the LORD DID SAY, was GO THIS WAY AND I WILL SHOW YOU. Abram was faithful and trusted in his LORD'S plan, *one step at a time.*

Our own faithful response to God indicates our love and trust for Him. When we hear God's call to *go and do,* we may not receive all the details at once. God provides *one day at a time,* and we can be sure that God's presence walks with us on our journey with Him.

PRAYER: Thank you, God, for your blessings and your plan for our lives. May we listen when you call and trust in You. Amen

NOTES:

THE JOURNEY

SCRIPTURE: Genesis 12:4b-9
KEY VERSE: Genesis 12:7

Do you remember as a kid getting impatient on a long trip? What was the question you recall asking? Yes! "Are we there yet?" It seems most of us like to get somewhere in a hurry, although if it is a long trip, then frequent stops for food, tourist attractions, bathrooms, or an overnight stay are helpful.

Abram had a lot to prepare for in order to journey from Haran to Caanan. He had possessions to pack up and there was his wife Sarai, and nephew Lot, plus all of the servants acquired in Haran. They took tents, household items, clothing, and livestock with them. They were also leaving memories behind as Abram's father Terah had died there. During their time in Haran they amassed some wealth. Haran was a prosperous caravan city and the LORD had surely blessed their stay.

The journey could not have been easy, and so they had stops along the way. However, the LORD'S blessings were with them on the trip. After finally arriving in Canaan, they stopped in Shechem at a sanctuary by the great tree of Moreh, where the LORD appeared to Abram. The locals worshipped pagan idols at this sanctuary, but Abram built an altar to the LORD. From there they pitched their tent east of Bethel, built an altar and prayed to the LORD. Then they headed toward the Negev to settle in the dry land south of Beersheba and eventually, due to famine in the land, ended up staying in Egypt.

Abram was always faithful to his LORD on this journey and was blessed. We can be faithful also, as we journey with God, knowing that He desires the best for us and is always with us. You may ask, "what am I doing in faithfulness to God? Will I be strong in the Lord and in the power of His might." That is your question to ponder.

PRAYER: Dear God, thank you for your word in scripture and for patriarchs like Abram who walked with You and were faithful. May I be faithful and continue the journey you have set for me. Amen

NOTES

EGYPT

Scripture: Genesis 12: 10-20
Key verse: Genesis 12:11-13

Ever move to a new and different town? How did you adapt? Different culture? Our family moved around a bit, so we knew firsthand about being a newcomer. When asked: "You're not from around here, are you?" Our positive reply was "No, but we got here as fast as we could!"

Abram and Sarai faced challenges when, due to the famine, they moved to Egypt. They had to be careful and navigate the culture. Abram recognized how beautiful Sarai was and knew the Egyptian practice of killing the husband in order to add a beautiful wife to Pharaoh's harem. Perhaps the couple agreed on a "playbook" ahead of time. Asking Sarai to say she was his sister may have been the most practical decision for them. That way Abram was safe from being murdered. Pharaoh took Sarai into his palace, but the scripture is silent on the situation. Problems began when disease hit Pharaoh's family. At a time when disease was considered an infliction due to wrongdoing, an angry Pharaoh confronted Abram for the truth. The result? Along with all the many gifts from Pharaoh, Abram and Sarai were kicked out of Egypt and returned to the Negev.

This is a thorny story with a difficult explanation. It provides a snapshot of the nature of their relationship as a couple, as well as the culture of the day. The LORD's role, it seems, was to inflict disease on the royalty in order to get the couple back home safely.

In life we may face awkward circumstances, sometimes created by ourselves. Be confident that our God remains patient with us and is never far away. Call on God for help when life gets complicated and ask for forgiveness when you may have contributed to the problem.

PRAYER: Heavenly Father, thank you for always watching over us, even when we get ourselves in awkward situations. Forgive me. We feel your presence, and we know you are never far away. Amen.

NOTES:

THE SEPARATION

SCRIPTURE: Genesis 13

KEY VERSE: Genesis 13:8-9

Ever used the technique of "separation" as a method to resolve conflict? Marriage counselors recommend it; business negotiators use it to make decisions. Separation from another when conflict is present can be a good strategy. It gives those in conflict " breathing space" so they can think about the best next steps. That is exactly what Abram and Lot decided to do. There was quarreling among their herdsmen because of the great number of flocks and herds for which they were responsible. The scripture tells us that the land was too small (including water and grasses) and just couldn't support them.

In this story we learn that Abram was a reasonable and kind man toward his nephew. He made no accusations or blame toward Lot or his herdsmen. Abram simply suggested that they part ways in order to have more room for growing possessions. Abram was generous in allowing Lot to make his own choice of land first. Emphasizing that they were family, he provided an opportunity for Lot to choose the good land of the Jordan up toward Sodom. Then Abram had faith that the LORD would define where he would settle.

The LORD spoke to Abram after Lot had departed and defined the covenant promise of land to him. The LORD asked Abram to look in all directions and then said that all that he could see would belong to him. Abram had faith in the covenant promise and moved to Hebron near the great trees of Mamre. Abram waited on the LORD to make his decisions on where to live.

When we are challenged and want to move ahead quickly on our own mortal decisions, it is a reminder to go to the LORD first, be patient and wait for the LORD's directions. That is a good plan.

PRAYER: Dear God, I have faith that you will always provide. When I make decisions about things in my life, I will pray and listen to your answer. Amen

NOTES:

KING AND PRIEST

SCRIPTURE: *Genesis 14*

KEY VERSES: *Genesis 14:18-20*

Ever had a brief encounter with someone you had never met before, and you never forgot it? Perhaps in the seat next to you on a plane, or in a store or on vacation? You might have wondered why, and what did it mean? Abram had just that, as he returned from a successful battle. He met and was blessed by someone he didn't know and had never met, whose name was Melchizedek, King of Salem and Priest of God Most High.

Abram, and his army, successfully fought four kings who attacked the kings of Sodom, Gomorrah, Admah, Zeboiim and Soar. Abram did this to rescue Lot, his nephew living in Sodom. Abram returned with goods, his nephew, Lot, his possessions, and family. They met with the King of Sodom in the Valley of Shaveh perhaps to celebrate and share part of their possessions.

King Melchizedek appears on the scene to bless Abram and shows his hospitality with bread and wine. Who was Melchizedek? Perhaps a Canaanite Priest, or worshipper of the one God "El"? Salem could be the name changed to Jerusalem. Could it be that Abram gave a tenth of everything he had to Melchizedek because he sensed they had the same God? Genesis provides no more information about this King and Priest. However, Psalm 110 and Hebrews 5 and 7 describe Melchizedek as *a type of Christ*, the King of Righteousness and Peace. Perhaps, in Genesis 14 we find a foreshadowing of the Messiah who is the Almighty Priest and King.

While we never can anticipate the encounters God places in our lives, we can imagine *why* we have met them and what it means. Perhaps we look back on the interaction and see the cause and the lesson. What did we learn from it? How did it impact us? What did it mean? I think God enjoys teaches us lessons. We must be observant.

PRAYER: Almighty God, your Word is perfect, providing joyful hints in the Old Testament of the Messiah. Bless us with wisdom to discern, as well as an open mind and heart to understand your revelations. Amen

NOTES:

ABRAM'S DOUBT

SCRIPTURE: Genesis 15
KEY VERSES: Genesis 15: 3- 4

It's August and we are in a heat wave. Our lawn is overgrown and overwatered. Frank, our dependable lawn guy, did not come. Conversation with my spouse goes like this:

Spouse: "I'm worried. Frank has not come by or called. I doubt he'll come now. It's too hot."

Me: "Yes, I think you should just cut the grass yourself. The grass is really high."

Spouse: "Yes, That's the best strategy."

Later Frank came, saw the mowed yard, and said: "Did you doubt me? Why didn't you call me? I'm always dependable. " Apologizing, we admitted we should have contacted him. We were wrong. How could we have doubted him?

Abram was doubting the LORD's promise of many offspring. Nothing was happening and time was running out. He and Sarai were aging and thought it impossible to have children. Yet the LORD kept telling Abram to look north, south, east and west to see all the land that would be his and his descendants. The LORD told him to count the stars, to estimate his many descendants. Abram probably thought, (my words) "I doubt this will happen."

So, Abram planned to bequeath his estate to his primary servant. What was the LORD's opinion about that? The LORD reminded Abram of His faithfulness, and dependability. He would surely receive a son from his own body. But Abram wanted a sign of a guarantee. How could Abram doubt? So, the LORD asked Abram to make a sacrifice to Him of a heifer, goat, ram, dove, and pigeon. Then, in a dream, the LORD spoke to Abram and appeared as a blazing torch coming down between the animal sacrifices. The LORD showed Abram His great power and with specific details renewed their covenant. He promised that Abram's descendants would receive the land from the Nile in Egypt to the Euphrates River.

We often doubt when we listen to the media and get different opinions of government leaders and those campaigning for national leadership. We tend to go to the negative when things are slow and when bad things happen. Our faith in God can encourage us. God is in control and is the LORD of the universe. Let us worship Him!

PRAYER: Dear God, we sometimes doubt that you are present in our lives. We attempt to take care of problems when we know we could come to you in prayer and hear your voice. Thank you for loving us and caring for every part of our days. Amen

NOTES

SARAI'S DOUBT

SCRIPTURE: Genesis 16: 1-6
KEY VERSES: Genesis 16:1-2

A young man in my congregation came to my study expressing bewilderment that God had not helped him get the job he thought he deserved. He had prayed for the job and thought God had let him down. I suggested the idea that perhaps God had something else in mind, and waiting on God might be useful. He rolled his eyes! Five months later he came by and was filled with excitement. God had indeed another plan for him. He had prayed for God's will to be done and waited with assurance. Now, he had accepted a position much better than he could ever have imagined. We prayed together thanking God for His perfect will.

Sarai was experiencing doubt that her LORD

would deliver on His promise. Abram was now 85 years old. It had been ten years since the LORD had told him to count the stars in the sky for their number of offspring. That promise had not yet become a reality. Doubt was still in the air. Sarai believed that her LORD had kept her barren, she was tired of waiting, and took matters into her own hands.

It was an ancient custom to use a maidservant as a surrogate in order to have a male heir if the wife could not conceive. *In theory*, that baby would belong to the first lady of the tent, the barren wife. Sarai decided to forego her LORD's promise and offered Hagar, her Egyptian maidservant, to Abram. The agreeable Abram slept with Hagar, and she conceived. The child from Hagar's womb was to belong to Abram and Sarai. Conflict grew between the pregnant Hagar and the barren Sarai. Sarai realized she had to rid herself of this boastful fertile maidservant. She blamed Abram and began mistreating Hagar until she fled the household.

Oh, we can be so obstinate! We want something our way, we try to fix it and when it doesn't work out, we accuse others of being the problem. That's our Sarai! And that is also us. Taking responsibility for our own decisions is an adult thing to do. We may make mistakes, but we can admit to them and take the consequences. Praying for a guide in decision making is a good thing. The Spirit of God is our guide.

PRAYER: Dear God, When I doubt you, I am showing my lack of faith. Forgive me. You are the Almighty and Loving Creator. Your timing is perfect, and your answers are a blessing. I will always trust you. Amen

NOTES:

CLOSE UPS

SCRIPTURE: *Genesis 16:7-15*
KEY VERSES: *Genesis 16:11,13a*

When we attended our granddaughter's university graduation, we located good seats in order to see her receive her diploma. Turns out the best view of her was on the big screen that hung from the ceiling of the arena. So, we took pictures of the big screen, as well as the actual event on stage! The pics of the big screen were her favorites as they were the best *close ups.*

Hagar wanted to be seen and heard. She was looking for something better in life. She had all she could take from Sarai's mistreatment, so she fled and found herself alone in the desert. We don't know what on earth she was thinking at the time, but guess she believed the desert was much better than being mistreated and the target of Sarai's anger and conflict. An angel of the LORD appeared to Hagar and also wondered what on earth she was thinking and asked where she was from and where she was going. A rather innocent pregnant Hagar answered simply that she was a lowly maidservant running away from the lady of the tent. The angel gave the good advice of returning and submitting, and also told her why.

The angel told Hagar that she would give birth to a son, name him Ishmael (God hears) and that his descendants would be too huge to count. Finally, Hagar felt heard and seen *close up by God* at this moment and she declared this experience out loud. Hagar had experienced the Holy One, and most likely carried the memory with her always. Hagar returned to Abram and Sarai. She bore Abram a son and named him Ishmael.

Sometimes it seems easier to just give up. So, we become depressed and saddened by what is happening in our lives rather than believing that the Holy One has the perfect answer for us. God always sees us *close up* and desires that we put our faith in Him.

PRAYER: Lord God, thank you for seeing me "close up." You love me and walk beside me all the days of my life. I give my days and my life to you. Amen

NOTES

NAME CHANGE

SCRIPTURE: *Genesis 17*

Key Verses: *Genesis 17:5*

The reason we give someone a name is important. If you have children, think of the process of choosing a first and middle name, and what it means to the family. Maybe you are named after a family member and are continuing the family legacy. Consider when someone marries today. Sometimes, the bride takes the groom's last name, or they hyphenate the last names of both. This makes a statement about the covenant of marriage where TWO become ONE. When we change our name, we change how we think of ourselves.

Why would God want to give new names to Abram and Sarai? Names are important to God because of their meaning. Sarah means "Princess" and Abraham means "Father of Many." The Almighty is making a *statement!* God changes how they think of themselves and defines their *roles and relationship* in His covenant with them. They become ONE in covenant as God's chosen *father and mother* of the nation of God's chosen people.

God had a great plan for His people and wanted them to be in covenant with Him. It is a two-way agreement with both parties giving to each other. As an example for ourselves, when we say we are children of God, then our part is to behave as a child of God. We are in covenant with God to be holy and righteous. We are in covenant and have been changed by the desire to follow the Almighty.

Have you ever chosen a nickname? I meet a number of people who have changed their names and when I ask why, they answer that the nickname was more like their own personality. They were not like the person they were named after. Of course, the reverse can apply. I like the idea of accepting the last name of my husband, but I kept my maiden name as a middle name. Somehow, I wanted to honor both. I like the idea of being a child of God, a King's Daughter. God is our Father God, and we are his children. I think that is worth remembering. We honor our God in all that we say and do.

PRAYER: Dear God, I want to covenant with you to be holy and righteous and to follow you day by day. Amen

NOTES:

COVENANT DETAILS

SCRIPTURE: *Genesis 17*

KEY VERSES: *Genesis 17: 9-10,13*

Some people love details, especially when it comes to managing finances: receipts, copies, budget, savings. They are the happiest checking on all that. They like it best when everything is in order, and they want to tell you about it. It is a good thing. Indeed, God's covenant with Abraham and Sarah had lots of details and *God wanted to share* what he had planned for Abraham, his family, and servants.

Genesis 17 records that God began His covenant requirements with the obligation for all males in Abraham's household to be circumcised. It was to be *a visible sign* that they belonged to God and in return He would offer them *protection, provision, and prosperity*. This act was meant to symbolize that the hearts of these men would be changed. When God spoke on that day, the entire male household was circumcised. Abraham was ninety years old, and Ishmael was thirteen. Abraham and his household were obedient.

Part of God's covenant conversation with Abraham was His blessing on Sarai, her name change and promise that she would give birth (at her advanced age) to a son, to be named Isaac, who would also be included in the covenant blessing. As a result, Sarah would become the mother of many peoples and nations. Abraham laughed at God's bold prediction for Sarah and asked for God's blessing for Ishmael. God vowed to make Ishmael the father of a great nation through twelve tribes. God also repeated and detailed the promise of Isaac's birth *within the year.*

God's covenant with Abraham and Sarah was now much clearer and more detailed. God meant business! He revealed his specific strategy and plan. *Today, God still wants the best for us, loves us, and offers us His protection, provision, and prosperity through Jesus Christ. That is worth exploring.*

PRAYER: *Thank you, Lord, for your relationship with us; and your good plans and blessings for each of us. Amen*

NOTES:

SARAH'S LAUGH

SCRIPTURE : Genesis 18: 1-15

KEY VERSES: Genesis 18: 13-15

Have you ever laughed sarcastically at an outrageous claim? Psychologists tell us that when a person laughs at something that seems impossible it's often a way to let go of fear or disbelief. If something sounds too good to be true, we laugh out loud. Sarah laughed in disbelief when she was told by visitors that she would give birth to a son at her advanced age of ninety. This is her story.

Abraham and Sarah are visited by three men who come to give a special message. The scripture (Genesis 18 and 19) implies that two of the men could have been angels and the third possibly the LORD himself. On their way to Sodom, the three visitors stop by, enjoy the hospitality of Abraham and Sarah, and give an unbelievable, seemingly impossible message to them. Sarah, in her tent at the time, heard the proclamation that within a year, she would give birth to a son. Like Abraham who laughed when God previously told him the same, Sarah laughed out loud!

Wonder what Sarah's laugh was like? Her tone? Was it a scoff? A sarcastic laugh? A belly laugh? Or was it a jump up and down praise, raise your hands to the Lord, rejoicing with thanks kind of laugh? You know the answer. It was a *"when pigs fly!!"* laugh. What would it take for Sarah to believe in the power of the Lord? When would she <u>really believe</u> that God loved her so much, and had plans just for her? Sarah still had doubt and little faith. The visitors heard her laugh and reminded the couple that nothing is too hard for the LORD.

Sometimes it is so hard to believe that God cares for us and has the power to bring about His Almighty plans for our lives. Like Sarah, we doubt, scoff, and maybe even laugh. A strong belief in the power of God is central to our faith. God was there in the beginning and is powerful now and ever. You can count on that!

PRAYER: Almighty God, thank you for loving me so much that nothing is too hard for you. Help my unbelief. Amen

NOTES

THE NEGOTIATION

SCRIPTURE: Genesis 18: 16-33

KEY VERSES: Genesis 18:20-21,23

When we hear or see the news these days, it seems that all around us we see wicked ways of people: theft, murder, slander, rape, cheating, lying. We might ask ourselves "what is going on in the world?" How can we stop all these wars, and the terrible ways people are treating one another? Sodom and Gomorrah were so wicked that today these cities are remembered and used to describe certain sexual acts.

The Bible illustrates how God responds to sinful behavior and to humans turning away from Him. As in the days of Noah, God was contemplating the destruction of Sodom and Gomorrah due to their grievous sin. Abraham, however, was concerned about those who were not participating in the sexual sin of their day. He had special concern, no doubt, for his nephew Lot and his family who lived in Sodom. Reminiscent of the flood story, God was saddened at the wicked ways of humans. He created a flood to destroy the world, yet saved Noah, his family, and two of every kind of animal. God had a different destruction in mind for Sodom and Gomorrah. And at Abraham's request, he saved one family.

Abraham was a persistent negotiator with God. He perhaps recalled the stories of the Great Flood, and how God saved a righteous family and renewed his covenant with mankind. Abraham pushed God to save the righteous ones. Repeatedly, he negotiated the required number of innocent people that God would save. Fifty? Forty? Thirty? Twenty? What if only ten? And God and Abraham settled on ten. Lot and his family would be saved.

God listens to our prayerful requests. Being bold, persistent, and earnest in our prayers to God is important. Sometimes God's timing is different from ours, and God's results are not exactly what we requested. However, when we pray in God's divine will, we discover that the results are given in His wisdom and love.

PRAYER: Dear Lord, thank you for listening to our persistent prayers. While you answer them according to your wise plan, you allow us to have a voice and an opinion. You hear us. Amen.

NOTES:

EVIL

SCRIPTURE: Genesis 19:1-29-

KEY VERSE: Genesis 19:29

God had a punishment in mind for Sodom and Gomorrah. And he saved one family. Evil sexual acts were rampant in the towns of Sodom and Gomorrah. God sent two angels to check on the status quo in Sodom where they met up with Lot and stayed the night with the family. Men who had gathered outside Lot's home began to shout for the two houseguests to come and have sex with them. Tension mounted, men were tearing down the front door, but Lot resisted. Troublesome though it sounds, Lot did offer his two virgin daughters to these evil men but was rejected. Clearly, they wanted the men. Recognizing the inevitable coming destruction God would bring upon Sodom, the angels protected Lot, his wife and daughters and they escaped the fire and damnation of punishment. Lot's wife, told not to look back, did the opposite, and turned into a pillar of salt.

Do we today have any evidence of this story of destruction? In our own travels, when we walked along the Dead Sea, not far from the archeological site of the ancient City of Sodom, our guide noted the presence of sulfur balls spread over the plains. Perhaps these sulfur balls resulted from earthquake activity? For that reason, the guide speculated that an ancient earthquake could have been responsible for destroying these cities of the plain. Also, nearby there are interesting salt formations that seem to take the form of a woman.

God expects us to have high moral standards. Stories of immorality in Genesis indicate that God punishes continued wrongdoing. Consider this, if you are a parent, you know how to discipline your child for wrongdoing. It hurts. You are saddened by the wrong behavior. Yet, as a parent we continue to love, hope, and pray for change in our children's behavior and teach them what is right and wrong. Scripture teaches that God loves us, provides second chances, and only uses dramatic consequences of punishment as a last solution.

PRAYER: *Dear God, thank you for creating and expecting a high moral standard for us. Forgive us when we are not the holy people You desire for us to be. Inspire us to stay strong in You. Amen*

NOTES:

LOT AND HIS DAUGHTERS

SCRIPTURE: Genesis 19: 30-38
KEY VERSE: Genesis 19: 36

When I was a teen, my father would frequently remind me that my choices and decisions in life always had consequences. He advised me to choose my friends carefully because "*you can become like those you surround yourself with.*" I offer only one reason possible for what Lot's daughters did to preserve the family line by having sex with their father. I believe the Sodom environment impacted their poor decisions and had lasting consequences.

How and why did these poor decisions come about? Recall when two angels arrived at Lot's home and the men of the town demanded to have sex with the two visitors. Lot's response was to show hospitable protection to the visitors and offered both his daughters as substitutes. Lot's low opinion of his daughters likely reflected the negative attitude toward women in Sodom and Gomorrah. Lot was influenced by his surroundings in an evil town.

Growing up in evil Sodom probably impacted Lot's daughters' decisions and contributed to their plan to sleep with their father in order to get pregnant. Also the daughters, living in the mountains with their father had no other man around to have as a husband. Lot, too, shares responsibility for these illicit acts, even though he is described as influenced by wine and unaware of the situation.

This story is difficult to digest. The bottom line is that we discover the _consequences_ of the daughters' choices. The daughters are impregnated by their father. Their sons, Moab and Ben-Ammi, become the fathers of the Moabites and the Ammonites. These two nations became bitter enemies of the descendants of Abraham.

In our own lives we must watch for our choices as they have consequences. When we have made those bad choices, then we must own up to them. In some cases we must pay the price, learn the lesson and ask for forgiveness from God and others.

PRAYER: Almighty God, thank you for your concern for our decisions. Help us to make wise choices. May they reflect your will in our lives. Amen

NOTES:

FEAR OF KING ABIMELECH

SCRIPTURE: Genesis 20
KEY VERSE: Genesis 20:13

Abraham and Sarah continued to travel to different regions in order to find fertile land for their livestock and any farming they wanted to do. They settled in Gerar in Philistine territory, near Gaza on the Mediterranean. Perhaps Abraham was surveying the land that God had promised to him. The scripture is silent on the reason for the settlement here, but clearly, he was to interact with the royal family and King Abimelech. This confrontation would be the beginning of future engagements. As in Egypt, Abraham asks Sarah to say she was his sister, in order to save Abraham from being killed by the King. God revealed the truth to King Abimelech so that he did not "touch" Sarah. Abraham found himself in trouble with the king who asked about his false story. Abraham explained that Sarah was his stepsister and he had told the truth.

Perhaps this repeated tale shows how God protected Sarah and Abraham each time they entered new territory. Despite Abraham's deception, the king blessed them with livestock, silver, and land for settlement. The two men would deal with each other again as they grappled with sharing the territory.

At times, human nature can rear its ugly head and cause us to make poor decisions. In this biblical story we again are shown Abraham's flaws in his faith. He tried to take charge of his fear of King Abimelech, instead of praying for God's protection. Then God intervened. God had made a covenant with Abraham to protect, provide and prosper him and his descendants.

We are being shown the human nature of Abraham and the lesson is clear: Relying on your own ideas and strategies can lead to negative consequences. God is your answer, and *You can count on God!*

PRAYER: Thank you, God, for your love, protection, and provision. We don't need to stand in your place. You are the Almighty One and we can trust in you. Amen

NOTES

LAUGHTER
WITH ISAAC

SCRIPTURE: Genesis 21: 1-7
Key Verse: Genesis 21: 6-7

Have you ever been overwhelmed at times by God's blessings and goodness toward you, your family and friends? We have! And, like Sarah, it was with the birth of grandbabies when we thought it to be impossible. We have been blessed when serious illnesses, like cancer, struck our family more than once, and family members were healed. I could write pages about God's goodness! Someday I will! And give God all the credit!

God was faithful and gave Sarah what He promised. Sarah was thrilled with her newborn and named him Isaac as God had instructed. Isaac means *laughter*. I imagine that Sarah jumped for joy, danced, and praised God! Contrast that laugh of joy with the disbelieving sarcastic *"when pigs fly laugh"* "she expressed from inside her tent, when God told her she would give birth in the upcoming year.

It is easier to thank God when His blessings continue to flow our way. It is harder when there are difficult or challenging times, and we have losses, or tragedy in our lives. That is when we need to pray harder, bow lower and believe that God is already at work ready to show us the good in life He has for us. Even then, God is already at work healing our hurts and wounds. Sarah had difficulty believing that one day she would be pregnant and tried to solve it herself without God. Was her faith weaker than we might expect? *Or was she like us?*

The beauty of Sarah is that she is <u>one of us</u>! She hurts, loves, laughs, cries, and gets angry just like we do! Her story is our story, yours and mine. May we rise up to honor and worship a God whose love for us is eternal.

PRAYER: Almighty God, thank you for your blessings, and your love, especially during our hard times. May we walk with you daily and may we see your goodness in all things. Amen

NOTES

TENSION AND DEPARTURE

SCRIPTURE: Genesis 21: 8-21
Key Verse: Genesis 21: 10-11

Life isn't always the way we'd like it to be. We tend to ask God "Why do bad things happen?" Divorce is a painful example especially when children are separated from one or the other parent. Lots of anger and tension between couples can exacerbate the problem. If you, or someone you know, has experienced divorce or separation, this Genesis story will have great meaning to you. Faith can provide comfort and insight. Yet it is not an easy journey.

In Genesis 21 we discover that everything was not "hunky dory" in the Abrahamic household. *Sarah was unhappy again.* Joy at the feast to celebrate the weaning of Isaac had turned into an angry moment for Sarah when Ishmael mocked his half-brother. She saw Ishmael as a threat to her son, Isaac, and especially a threat to Isaac's inheritance.

As tensions escalated, Sarah demanded that Abraham *get rid of* Hagar and Ishmael. Surely, Abraham was distressed by her request because he loved his son, Ishmael. God reminded Abraham that he would care for Ishmael and make him into a great nation. Abraham offered water and food for Hagar and Ishmael's journey and said a brief goodbye. God watched over Hagar and Ishmael as they wandered in the desert of Beersheba, providing spring water when they cried out and assured them of the great nation that would come from Ishmael. The scripture tells us that God was present throughout Ishamel's life. He lived in the Desert of Paran and married an Egyptian woman.

It is hard when bad things happen. Abraham's faith provided comfort and strength to handle this separation. When we hurt, we can pray for the condition we and others are experiencing. God can be our comfort and guide.

PRAYER: Dear God, comfort me and help me to depend on You for my understanding. Amen

NOTES:

ABIMELECH AND THE TREATY

SCRIPTURE: Genesis 21:22-34
KEY VERSE: Genesis 21:34

The character of a person is important. Sometimes we refer to that as *credibility*. It means that you are trustworthy, hardworking, and capable. When you interact with another person you do so with interest, knowledge, and trust. Those characteristics are important in relationships. Abraham needed to show those characteristics to King Abimelech especially after earlier using a "little white lie" about his relationship to Sarah.

Seems like a treaty between the two would be a good idea for building relationships. Afterall, Abraham and Sarah were living in a Philistine area where people did not trust strangers. King

Abimelech wanted assurance that he would be dealt with honestly and Abraham desired the King's help in adjudicating conflict over a well with the King's servants. Certainly, time for a treaty was at hand. To prove himself a reliable friend Abraham brought livestock to show his kindness to the King. That was his treaty ceremonial gift to the King and they both swore an oath of friendship that day. They named the place Beersheba, which means "well" indicating their capacity to solve the issue at hand.

Today, we generally do not solve personal issues with a treaty but might use legal help if needed. We might agree to disagree and may often give a friend a gift or money to solve a disagreement. Culture required a more legal manner in ancient times. Giving physical items was a way of paying for the problems and the issues. Abraham even planted a tree to memorialize the treaty. This story illuminates Abraham's character and desire to treat others well. We can learn from Abraham and follow his example.

When we disagree with others, it is best to solve it, as those issues tend to cast a negative shadow over our relationships. God gives grace to us, and we can share it with others.

PRAYER: Thank you, God, for the example of Abraham as he dealt with others in his life. Help us to be people of Godly character treating others well. Amen

NOTES:

THE TEST

SCRIPTURE: Genesis 22: 1-19

KEY VERSE: Genesis 22:2

This story is so emotional, incredible, and hard to believe. To be told to kill your own son is abominable. Why would God test Abraham this way? Did Abraham believe God would save Isaac? Abraham followed God's directions, travelled to Moriah, bound Isaac, laid him on the sacrificial altar, and was taking up his knife when *God intervened* and provided a ram as a substitute. Then God told Abraham that due to his obedience, he and his descendants would be blessed.

Wonder if it crossed Abraham's mind to question God and ask, (my words) *'How many times do I have to prove myself to You, Lord, in order to show I am faithful?'* Abraham followed all of God's directions from the moment God called him in Haran. Years of being obedient, talking with God, experiencing His blessings, losing Ishmael, circumcising all the Abrahamic male household, enduring the conflicts of Hagar and Sarah, and then to be *tested with the sacrifice of Isaac?*

I am weaker than Abraham. It might have crossed my mind to say to God: *"Sorry, I draw the line here."* Am I a woman of little faith? Am I part of the same human struggle with obedience as were Adam and Eve? Here Abraham is a role model for us because he was obedient to God *in all things and God provided.*

The real truth is *It was God's plan all along.* A ram was a substitute offering so Isaac could live. God was foreshadowing His plan for *His only Son* to be an obedient offering on the cross. Jesus was a substitute offering for our sins resulting in a new way of life for us.

When you are tested repeatedly by difficult circumstances, remember God's love is profound, present and you're not alone. *God has already come before your difficulty. He has had a plan in place for you, all along.*

PRAYER: *God, I know you are ever present, and you love me. When I hurt or question my circumstances, I will trust in you. I will show my faithfulness in all things. Amen*

NOTES:

SARAH'S DEATH

SCRIPTURE: *Genesis 23*
KEY VERSE: *Genesis 23: 1-2*

My mother passed away several years before my father, and I recall watching him stand over her open casket at the front of the church. She looked beautiful, all made up and her hair fixed so perfectly. She was wearing a lovely blue green dress and her pearl necklace and earrings which were her favorites. My father had his "I'm not going to cry" face on but that didn't last long as he told her goodbye, and what a wonderful wife and mother she had been. Later we gathered at the family cemetery. After a brief service, we walked among the headstones identifying "who was who" from the long list of relatives buried there. Burials and grave markers are important for family memories and to say "goodbye."

In ancient times burying the deceased was often done in a family cave or on the property of the deceased. Abraham no doubt wanted the very best for his beloved Sarah. She had been his support and had given him a son, Isaac, to continue God's promise. After all the years of married life, I think that Abraham probably had his "I'm not going to cry" face on too. She would be buried in the cave of Machpelah in Hebron, near Mamre. This site was so important to Abraham that he offered to pay the owner, Ephron the Hittite, full price for both the field and the cave in it. Later it would also become the burial site for Abraham, Isaac and Rebekah, Jacob, and Leah.

Here in this story we get yet another glimpse of the character of Abraham, who loved his wife and family, was faithful to God, and was blessed because of his faith. He is a role model for patriarchs to follow and for us today. Today it is up to us to honor those who came before us, and who sacrificed their lives for us and others. We are part of a bigger family than we can imagine. It is the family of God, and as His children we honor and remember one another.

PRAYER: Thank you, God, for Sarah who served you well and is a role model for women today. We appreciate her feisty side and her dedication to Abraham and Isaac. She supported Abraham's calling, even to the point of saying she was "his sister" to keep him safe. She was a faithful follower of You, God. Thank you for her life and heritage. Amen

NOTES

ISAAC

A WIFE FOR ISAAC

SCRIPTURE: *Genesis 24*

KEY VERSE: *Genesis 24:4*

How does one choose someone to marry? In the United States, people can be free to choose a mate, but this is not true of all. Depending on the traditions of the family, religion, or country of origin, choosing a mate can involve more decision makers. In 2000 BCE it was likely to be a parent or matchmaker to negotiate on the son's behalf. Such was the case when Abraham sent his servant to locate a bride for Isaac from his ancestral line. Get ready for a great romantic story, where you might say "this was meant to be!" God had a plan!

On his way to Nahor to find a wife for Isaac, the servant took gifts from Abraham's household to impress the family; to showcase Isaac's wealth. Upon arriving, the servant sat beside the town's spring, and asked God for the right woman to come and offer him a drink and water his camels. Rebekah arrived and did just that. As the answer to prayer, she came with family ties, beauty, and virginity. The traditional family negotiation was decided favorably. Rebekah was to be the wife of a wealthy man.

The first meeting of Rebekah and Isaac seems like a movie scene. Rebekah and her entourage had traveled to meet Isaac when she spotted him in a field walking toward her. Probably blushing, Rebekah took her veil and covered herself. Was it love at first sight? I think I can sense God smiling, can you? Isaac was given a beautiful wife. She comforted him and he loved her.

The Almighty knows how to bring us joy in many ways. For Isaac, at this moment in time, it was Rebekah. God may have given you the gift of joy in a person you now love. Thank God for your beautiful circumstances and the people in your life.

PRAYER: Loving God, thank you for your blessings. In times of trial and temptation, help me to remember the love and joy from you. I am grateful for your goodness, Oh God. Amen

NOTES:

INHERITORS OF
THE COVENANT

SCRIPTURE: Genesis 25: 1-18
Key Verses: Genesis 25: 7-9

Ancestry history is flourishing in our culture. A variety of companies have software to connect us to our ancestors from hundreds and thousands of years before us. We discover the national origins of those who came before us. Just take a DNA test and you can uncover families and countries no relative ever told you about. I was bursting with pride when I discovered through my research online that I had ancient royalty, writers, founding fathers and founders of colleges in my DNA. I even identified the ships they took to the newfound America! My pride was shattered when I also uncovered murderers, witches, fornicators, lunatics, and thieves in my ancestral history. We are a colorful family!

As we explore the Abrahamic descendants, we will find dual accounts of blessings and prosperity as well as sins of jealousy and deceit. Genesis 25 provides the names of the descendants of Abraham through Ishmael and Isaac. An often-surprising person mentioned is Keturah, Abraham's wife after Sarah died. Keturah bore six sons to whom Abraham gifted part of his fortune and sent them eastward to be apart from Isaac. They prospered and had many descendants. Abraham left everything else to Isaac. Abraham died at the old age of 175 years and his sons buried him in the family burial site, the Cave of Machpelah beside Sarah.

Ishmael, son of Abraham and Hagar, prospered and lived 137 years. Settling near the Egyptian border, Ishmael's sons became the leaders of twelve tribes, just as God had promised Hagar. Some of the sons' names listed in Genesis 25: 12-18 reflect the tradition that Ishmael was the father of the Arabs. Genesis 25: 18 notes that they experienced conflict with others around them.

God's covenant with Abraham continues with

Isaac, son of Abraham and Sarah, and his handpicked wife Rebekah, the daughter of Bethuel and sister of Laban. The story continues.

PRAYER: *Dear God: Thank you for our families. Sometimes we ourselves are the good, the bad and the ugly, yet you love each and every one of us. Help us to see the beauty in our own families despite our disagreements and differences. May we understand how we can love our families better. Amen*

NOTES:

TWINS

SCRIPTURE: *Genesis 25: 19-28*

KEY VERSES: *Genesis 25:21-23*

A pregnant woman knows what it is like to feel her unborn baby move inside her body. Sometimes it is as simple as hiccups or kicking movements while she is listening to loud music, watching TV, or trying to go to sleep. A husband knows what it is like for his wife to take his hand and place it on her tummy, as she smiles and says: "Can you feel that?"

Rebekah was having trouble getting pregnant. Isaac prayed for her to have children and God answered his prayers. However, the pregnancy was not going well, and was uncomfortable for Rebekah. Scripture describes that Rebekah had excessive activity in her womb while pregnant, and asked God what was going on. God informed her she had two nations in her womb that would be in conflict. Those twins were already "duking" it out in the womb. The twin boys were very different in looks and temperament. Esau, the firstborn had lots of red hair that covered his body, love for hunting and the outdoors, and he was his father Isaac's favorite. Jacob, the second born, was a quiet person, a homebody of sorts and was his mother Rebekah's favorite.

The twins' differences and parents' favoritism of different sons had the power to create conflict between sons as well as tension between the parents. A crisis was brewing that would cause harm and hurt to the family. Stay tuned as we soon will observe the family conflict of Isaac, Rebekah, Jacob, and Esau.

Conflict in a family is sad, overwhelming, and heartbreaking. When you experience it, you pray for help from God to give you the words and solutions to handle and resolve it. God loves families and desires to help you confess, forgive, and love one another.

PRAYER: *Almighty One, we cry out to you and pray for your help. Give us the words and the heart to forgive one another and to live in peace and harmony in our family. Amen*

NOTES

DESPISED BIRTHRIGHT

SCRIPTURE: *Genesis 25: 29-34*
KEY VERSES: *Genesis 25: 33-34*

Today, people often rely on their Last Will and Testament and Trust to declare what happens with their land, home, and valuables after their death. Attorneys and financial experts are involved, and lists are made of names, belongings, and shares. It is a legal, written document, signed and notarized. All involved have a copy and the original is kept in the bank safe deposit box in the owner's name to be read upon death, usually by the family's attorney.

Inheritance was a two-step process in the ancient world. First, according to custom, the birthright inheritance was intended to be given to the eldest son, and then later followed by the father's final deathbed *spoken* blessing on the same son. The value of the spoken word in this culture was paramount. You honored and kept your spoken promises. The Abrahamic covenant promises with God were clear. Passed from eldest son to eldest son, each inherited God's promises to protect, provide and prosper the family. Esau was the firstborn son and in the covenant line from Isaac. That covenant relationship included both the concept of *the birthright and the blessing* from the patriarch. It was an honorable oral agreement.

It took just a nano second for Esau to give away his birthright. How did it happen? Esau had come in from hunting declaring that he was starving and needed something to eat immediately! Jacob had made lentil stew and Esau demanded to be served on the spot! Jacob agreed to serve him but only if Esau would hand over his birthright in exchange. Esau apparently was so famished that he agreed. *It was a sworn oral agreement. The birthright was now Jacob's.* Esau finished off the lentil stew without a thank you and left. Maybe the birthright wasn't that important to Esau at the time. Or did Jacob take advantage of the situation to get what he wanted from Esau? The story continues.

Have you ever been tricked or deceived? How does it feel? What happens when we deceive someone, and we get what we want by taking advantage of others?

PRAYER: Dear God, thank you for being in my heart. When I have been deceived, it is hard to believe because I trusted the deceiver. Give me grace, forgiveness and understanding. Amen.

NOTES:

GOD BLESSES ISAAC

SCRIPTURE: Genesis 26

KEY VERSES: Genesis 26: 1-3

Ever had ongoing conflict with someone? No matter what you tried to do, conflict was always present? The Philistine people around Isaac were looking for a fight. Isaac obeyed God and stayed in Gerar in the land of the Philistines and God blessed him with abundant crops, flocks, herds, and servants. Isaac's presence in Gerar was not welcome, perhaps due to his wealth, or his worship of a God people did not understand. Isaac was considered a threat. Due to the famine, there were fights over water and wells that had been dug in the dry land. Just like today, we see conflict over water, oil, land, power, or religion.

Isaac didn't want to get involved in the conflict

over the wells and water. Also tension had erupted because of Isaac's falsehood to Abimelech that his wife, Rebekah, was his sister (a clear repeat of his father, Abraham's, debacle). It became impossible to function with the friction. At Abimelech's request Isaac moved from the quarrelling and settled in Beersheba. There Isaac set up an altar and thanked the LORD for his safety. Later, Abimelech requested a peace treaty between them because he saw that God was with Isaac .

God was at work protecting and blessing Isaac, just as he protected Abraham. Isaac trusted God just as his father Abraham had. God comforted Isaac by reminding him of his Abrahamic covenant to protect, provide and prosper.

Relationships can be very difficult sometimes. God cares for us and can help us navigate the issues and problems. Our faith can keep us focused on God and not on the conflict.

PRAYER: Dear God, when conflict occurs, teach me to trust you. Guide me to listen to your voice and to not be afraid. Amen

NOTES:

THE DECEIT

SCRIPTURE: *Genesis 27: 1-18*
KEY VERSES: *Genesis 27: 8-10*

This story is fraught with favoritism, jealousy, deceit, manipulation, and grief. Families torn apart; spouses in conflict. Little did Isaac ever expect, when he and Rebekah first looked lovingly into each other's eyes many years earlier, that this would occur. Rebekah, in Hebrew, means "captivating" or "snare." A hint all along!

This drama unfolds with Rebekah hatching a plan for Jacob to receive Esau's rightful blessing. You will recall that the elder son receives the birthright inheritance automatically as well as the blessing spoken by the father. According to this story, Esau had despised his birthright and given it away to Jacob for a bowl of lentil stew and bread. All Jacob needed now was the blessing from his father, Isaac.

Rebekah went to work being deceitful. She was determined to bypass Esau and work on behalf of her favorite son, Jacob. She heard Issac tell Esau to prepare to receive his blessing, and to bring his father's favorite wild game meal. So Rebekah was sneaky. She ordered Jacob to get two choice goats and *she* prepared Isaac's favorite stew. Then she dressed Jacob in Esau's clothes and covered his smooth hands and neck with goat skins to simulate Esau's hairy skin. She went ALL OUT to make this charade work. To Jacob's credit he told his mother he was hesitant to pretend he was Esau, thinking of the consequences if his father discovered the charade. What was Rebekah's response? Basically (in my words) she said: *"don't worry about it!"* She would take the fall if necessary! Jacob was about to become someone he was not. Grab a tissue. This story continues.

It is deceitful to pretend you're somebody or something that you are really not. Maybe the façade is wealth, status, intellect, kindness, or beauty, and you want to impress. Ego can be a hurtful thing for us, our friends, family and acquaintances. God created us and desires that we show the world the real person that we have become in God's grace and love.

PRAYER: Forgive me, God, when I have treated someone disrespectfully. Guide me to love and respect others. Amen.

NOTES:

THE STOLEN BLESSING

SCRIPTURE: *Genesis 27:19-40*
KEY VERSE: *Genesis 27:38*

Family dynamics are interesting especially when there is competition between siblings. In the case of Esau and Jacob each one was favored by a different parent, so the competition was actually between the parents. We know precious little of Isaac and Rebekah's marriage relationship. Even reading between the lines, we are left with some fuzzy suggestions. The following ideas are my own.

Isaac was an only child, being raised by older parents who may have doted on him. Isaac married a young Rebekah after his mother Sarah had died . As a young wife, Rebekah comforted Isaac; he loved her and prayed for her when she had a hard time getting pregnant. The twins were long anticipated, and each parent hung onto their favorite. Perhaps inside an aging marriage both parents needed attention and love from their chosen twin. An aging Isaac was losing his eyesight and near death. Rebekah turned to her favorite son to get what she wanted for him. Jacob really had no choice and followed his mother's devious plan.

Identifying himself as Esau, Jacob deceived his father with a kiss. Isaac, responding to the smell of Esau's clothes that Jacob wore, unknowingly blessed his younger son. *The deed was done. The blessing was stolen from Esau. It was permanent and unchangeable.* When Esau returned from hunting to greet his father and receive the blessing, he realized the deceit. This heartbreaking moment culminates with Esau's crying plea to his father for an additional blessing. The dying Isaac's response was that it was too late. Imagine Esau's pain. Though he had given away his birthright inheritance, he believed he deserved his father's blessing. This story is littered with questions. *Was this part of God's plan? Was Rebekah unknowingly or knowingly fulfilling God's prophecy that the older twin would serve the younger. And Esau?* The story continues.

What is our lesson here? Fairness is not always distributed evenly. Deceit hurts both the deceived and the deceiver. We can have hope that a loving God is fair. Our understanding takes faith and time for God to show us His perfect will.

PRAYER: Dear God, we are confused sometimes by what happens around us and to us. Help us to understand and trust in you. Amen

NOTES

THE GRUDGE

SCRIPTURE: Genesis 27: 41-46;
Genesis 28: 1-9
KEY SCRIPTURE: Genesis 27:41

Remember the story of the Hatfield's and McCoy's who hated each other? The neighborhood knew about it, but few could recall what started the feud. Some families were so angry that they no longer spoke even if they were in the same room. The reason for the conflict is told differently by all involved. Instead of problem solving, they hold a grudge, or cause the other party to have pain. *"Getting even"* is what I call it!

Esau held a grudge against his family and may have thought (my words): "Jacob has left town, so I cannot kill him. I will get even with my parents who are to blame, too. I will hurt them just like they have hurt me. They will hate it if I marry a Canaanite woman." So Esau married a Canaanite woman, Ishmael's daughter, Mahalath.

I believe that both Esau and Jacob had been emotionally hurt because of parental favoritism. This unhealthy environment created jealousy and hatred between the twins. Rebekah had worked her magic to hurt and reject Esau in favor of Jacob. The pain from rejection was Esau's to bear. We are not told how Rebekah and Isaac handled this conflict in their marriage except to send Jacob away to keep him safe from Esau's wrath. Perhaps they just avoided the conflict and agreed to never discuss it again. Rebekah convinced Isaac to send Jacob to Paddan Aram, to the home of her brother, Laban in order to select a wife from his daughters. She desperately did not want Jacob to marry a Canaanite woman!

We all have choices on how we handle conflicts in our lives. Some like to talk it to death; others just bury the conflict, hoping and praying it will never happen again. Seeking professional help is a good option, as is separation from the conflict situation. Prayer also helps calm us, as we put our issues in God's hands.

Read on! More deception is coming, and Jacob gets his comeuppance in Laban's house.

PRAYER: Dear God, I am weary of conflict. Help me let go of my anger and find better ways to improve my relationships. Help me love one another. Amen

NOTES

JACOB

STAIRWAY TO HEAVEN

SCRIPTURE: *Genesis 28:10-22*

KEY VERSES: *Genesis 28:12-13,15*

Do you dream when you are sleeping? Many people say that they don't recall their dreams. Others describe vivid dreams that are unforgettable and impact their lives. Here is Jacob's story about a dream experience that *changed him forever.*

Having left the home of his parents, Jacob was on a journey to Rebekah's homeland and her brother Laban's home to find a wife. On this journey, Jacob stopped to rest for the night and had a dream of a stairway to heaven with angels ascending and descending. Above it stood the LORD who spoke to Jacob promising to continue the Abrahamic covenant through him and his descendants. Previously, Jacob referred to the LORD as the God of his father, Isaac. Now, this LORD was *his* God.

Jacob would be taking up the mantel of God's covenant with Abraham and, like his father and grandfather, he would have a close walk with the LORD. God's promise to never leave Jacob is his expression of love. He promised Jacob protection, provision, and prosperity. Jacob knew that the presence of the LORD was in this place. To commemorate he put a stone there as a pillar of worship and renamed the city Bethel, which means the house of God.

Jacob had encountered the Almighty for himself and it was lifechanging. It is no accident that the LORD revealed himself *before* Jacob arrived at Laban's home. Jacob was being strengthened to grow in his faith and handle the upcoming events that he would experience. Also, God had gone ahead and chosen the women that Jacob would marry. He was firmly in God's hands.

We, too, can experience the spirit of the living God in our everyday lives. The Almighty goes before us, and walks with us, setting our paths straight. And that can change us forever.

PRAYER: Thank you, God, for your presence, just as you spoke to Abraham, Isaac, and Jacob. The presence of your Spirit reminds me that I belong to You. You will always love me and be with me. Amen

NOTES:

LOVE AND DECEIT

SCRIPTURE: Genesis 29: 1-30
Key Verses: Genesis 29:26-27

Jacob arrived near Haran, his mother's homeland, and stopped to visit with the locals at the well. What is it about meeting folks at the well? Maybe a little like conversation around the water cooler at work? Appears there are beautiful women who come to the well. And it is obvious by now that the men of the covenant seem to appreciate and select beautiful women! Sure enough, God was at work, and an incredible Rachel came to the well to water her livestock. For Jacob it was love at first sight!

Laban (Jacob's uncle) invited Jacob to stay with the family and go to work for him. To work and see the love of your life everyday was a treat for Jacob. Could life get any better? Now, unsurprisingly, Jacob asked Laban for Rachel as his wife. The deal struck was if Jacob worked for Laban for seven years, then in return, he could marry Rachel.

The bride, hiding under traditional ancient covering, was the fruition of all that Jacob desired. However, Jacob's idea of a honeymoon following the wedding feast was deceitfully micro-managed by Laban. Jacob did not realize who he had taken as a wife until the following morning when Jacob rolled over to kiss his bride. Surprised, he looked into the eyes of Leah, Rachel's older sister, the woman he had slept with. What deceit! Laban's excuse? The eldest must marry first. Finish the bridal week with Leah, then Jacob could have Rachel also. The price? Work for Laban for another seven years!

The irony of it! Jacob, who had deceived his brother Esau and father Isaac, was now deceived himself. Was this a lesson for Jacob? Think so! *What goes around, comes around.*

The Almighty teaches us lessons in a variety of ways. Many times we have to experience for ourselves the pain we have inflicted on others. Then we begin to understand and change our ways.

PRAYER: Dear God, when we hurt others, we pay a price for our sinful behavior. It is the way we learn. Thank you for your forgiveness, teaching, and love. Amen

NOTES

JEALOUSY

SCRIPTURE: *Genesis 29-30:1*

KEY VERSE: *Genesis 30:1*

Jealousy is the theme of Genesis with Cain and Abel, Hagar and Sarai, Esau and Jacob. All competed for love, attention, and approval. People were hurt; bad things happened. It's not so different in our culture today. Our lives are complicated just as in ancient times. For Leah and Rachel the complication was that Jacob had to care for multiple wives and maidservants. We can draw a parallel between their lives and ours, today. Conflict and jealousy can flare during divorces and multiple marriages which produce stepchildren, stepparents, and step siblings. When handled inappropriately, jealousy and competition can erupt and harm families. We might criticize the

Genesis families and then fail to recognize similarities in our society today.

Leah and Rachel competed for the love of Jacob. Leah's words ring so true after she gave birth to Jacob's first son and mused that perhaps Jacob would now love her. Bearing children was an important part of a woman's life in the ancient world; it brought love and societal respect. In a short span of time Leah gave birth to four sons: Reuben, Simeon, Levi, and Judah! Rachel's cry of desperation that she might die if Jacob didn't make her pregnant reminds us of the impact being childless had on ancient women.

What continued was a hefty competition between Leah and Rachel to have children. One solution was to give one's maidservants to Jacob as a wife to impregnate. This approach resulted in two more sons (Gad and Asher) for Leah through her maidservant (Zilpah) and two sons for Rachel (Dan and Naphtali) through her maidservant (Billah).

We can learn from their mistakes and evaluate our own lives. Jealousy offers no good news. What is the Good News? That we are ALL loved by our Creator and accepted into the world of Creation. Can we truly love God, ourselves, and others ? Can we reside in a world of acceptance and individuality. I think so. I pray so.

PRAYER: *Dear God, thank you for describing the families in Genesis. You shared the truth about the human condition. It is not our accomplishments that cause you to love us. We are your TREASURE because you created us. Thank you for your LOVE. Amen.*

NOTES:

147

MANDRAKES

SCRIPTURE: *Genesis 30:14-24*
KEY VERSE: *Genesis 30:14*

How far will you go when you are jealous of someone and what they have? You buy things you can't afford? Do you copycat someone's wardrobe or home décor? Buy a new truck when the one you have will do? Or maybe gaslight or complain about them with friends? Seems Jacob's wives were still having trouble in the jealousy department. No matter if you confessed your jealousy right now, I could assure you that you don't have anything over on these women. They are the best in the world! Truly, I laugh out loud when summarizing this Genesis story. The theme is competition and how far Leah and Rachel will go to be the best at producing children. It is the story of *who gets the mandrakes?* I'll start at the beginning.

The mandrakes were a gift to Leah from her son Reuben, who found them in the field. These plant roots, when eaten, are believed to be magical and help cause pregnancy because they resemble the shape of the human lower anatomy. Rachel saw the mandrakes that Leah received and demanded her rightful share. Leah declined. To settle this dispute the sisters agreed to share the mandrakes and share sleeping with Jacob. Leah was first up! Imagine for a moment being Jacob and being told that he must sleep with his wives on alternate nights. The outcome? Leah became pregnant and bore Jacob's fifth son, Issachar, then a sixth son, Zebulun; and a daughter, Dinah. Then Rachel gave birth to a son, Joseph. Did the mandrakes work? That's for you to decide.

The real lesson here is that we don't need to run ahead of God. Somehow, we feel the need to make stuff happen. Waiting for God's timing often is frustrating and takes too long. Trusting in God was difficult for Sarah, Rebekah, Leah and Rachel. It's the human condition. These stories are important because they are about us! Trusting in God's timing and perfect will shows that we are ready to put our lives in God's hands. God has the perfect plan for us.

PRAYER: Thank you, God, for loving us so much that you have the perfect plan for us. We simply have to put our trust in you. Amen

NOTES:

AFFLUENCE AND
TRICKERY

SCRIPTURE: Genesis 30:25-43
KEY SCRIPTURE: Genesis 30: 31-32

I know nothing about breeding sheep. On a Scotland tour we observed these animals, and the guide explained that when a breeder wanted pure white lambs, they would isolate the white sheep from the spotted, speckled, and striped ones. Even in isolation, the genes in the DNA could still produce non-white lambs. Also a lamb could be black at birth; yet later their fleece could become white. Seems to me that breeding can be complex.

Jacob understood the science of breeding these animals. He wanted independence from Laban, so he needed his own identifiable sheep. Jacob suggested to Laban that he would take the marked sheep for his own by culling them from Laban's flocks. Joseph believed in an ancient magical notion that images observed at conception could be transferred to the offspring. Therefore, Jacob exposed speckled and spotted tree limbs to the livestock when they came to mate and drink at the watering trough. Since he was paid wages based on the number of spotted and speckled livestock he raised, volume was the plan! They multiplied and Jacob became wealthy. But he was fighting an uphill battle with Laban.

Laban was a trickster also. He culled his own flocks of the spotted and speckled livestock and transferred them to his sons for care. Two tricksters deceiving one another! *What's the lesson here? Once again, deceit never works.* Laban and his sons were turning on Jacob. Jacob knew to survive and thrive his departure had to be soon. He needed God.

The lesson? The game of trickery is a lesson nobody can win. Trusting one another is the key to good relationships. Caution in relationships is valuable if there are repeated incidents in your encounters with others. Pray about it and listen to your Father in Heaven.

PRAYER: Dear God, thank you for providing your wisdom. When I am at odds with another person, I must turn to you. Help me look honestly at myself and my role in the tension between others and myself. Help me learn from my negative actions and encounters. Forgive me for harming others. Amen

NOTES:

FLIGHT TO GILEAD

SCRIPTURE: Genesis 31:1-21

KEY SCRIPTURE: Genesis 31: 3

We love to travel! My dear spouse and I have driven, walked, cruised, hiked, bussed, and flown to many parts of the globe. It's hard, but worth the effort, especially when you are flying home to see family. That moment when you see your family is worth all the effort of travel. We just recently gathered our family to remember the life of my husband's mother, my sweet, dear mother-in-law. A professional photographer documented the event. That family photo hangs in our home as a most precious memory. It was a special time.

Jacob must have been filled with emotion as he gathered all of his family and *started home*. It was a huge trip from Haran across Paddan Aram to

Canaan. It would take weeks to get home. I think Jacob must have been relieved *to actually flee* from Laban. Lots of memories of heartache, deceit, jealousy, loss, sadness may have flooded Jacob's mind. But *going home* had to be the greatest motivator to make such a long trip with so many people and things: wives, children, concubines, maidservants, shepherds, nurses and then the livestock, personal items, tents, household items, clothing, precious memorabilia. The promise that God was protecting and providing must have comforted Jacob and his entourage. Afterall it was God's idea to go home. So, Jacob planned his first stop, in Gilead.

For us, going home after living far away is personal and emotional. Visiting your childhood home, walking through your old high school, eating at a favorite college hideaway can bring a flood of memories to be thankful for. I think that God must like it when we thank Him for the life he has provided.

PRAYER: God, thank you for our family and friends, for all those we hold dear. Thank you for protection and provision and for the memories of family and friends who are no longer with us. Amen.

NOTES:

PURSUIT AND DECEIT

SCRIPTURE: Genesis 31: 22- 42

KEY SCRIPTURE: Genesis 31: 27-28

Ever been so upset with someone that you just had to confront them? Maybe they kept your children out too late at a birthday party. Or your daughter's date took her to the wrong kind of club. Or your boss failed to update you on important information you needed. You just HAD to express your reaction. The WAY you confronted the offense was important. That was the case for Laban who was angry because Jacob had secretly left and taken his family with him.

This heated story is full of passion, confusion and chaos. After locating Jacob, Laban had something to say. He needed answers. Why? What was Jacob thinking? Would his daughters and grandchildren be safe? Questions came hotly. The answer Jacob gave

Laban who asked "why" was that he feared his family would be taken away from him.

Is that really what was on Laban's mind? The conversation shifted. In the middle of this query, Laban's real concern took center stage: "*Who stole his household gods?*" Did they have greater importance to Laban than the family departure? What a spectacle as Laban searched the family tents for his gods and found nothing. Laban was never going to find his pagan gods, because Rachel, the culprit, had stolen them and put them inside her camel's saddle where she was sitting. Rachel lied, telling her father that she could not stand for she was unclean due to her time of the month. Why the theft? Angry with her father? Needing pagan protection? Last minute takeaway? We'll never know. No pagan gods found. Laban's priority issue goes unsolved. Jacob had hit his limit, saying everything to Laban he had been holding back all these years. Hopefully it made him feel better.

This covenant family can be bewildering. Are they *dysfunctional*? Was that even a term in the Ancient World? These stories remind us that we are imperfect, too. In spite of our frailties, God keeps loving us and helping us accomplish His perfect will. Something to ponder!

PRAYER: *Thank you, God, for your love and grace. In spite of our imperfections you call upon us to rise up and cooperate with you to change the world in your name. Amen*

NOTES:

COVENANT OF INDEPENDENCE

SCRIPTURE: Genesis 31:43-55
KEY VERSES: Genesis 31:49

Possibly every parent alive today can recall the place in the wedding ceremony, where they were asked to give away a son or daughter to the person chosen to be their forever spouse. I admit that I cried every time. The separation of young adults from their parents marks an important development, because they need to be independent. Jacob was ready to be independent, become the head of his own family, and to follow in the footsteps of his father and grandfather.

This covenant of independence was critical for both Jacob and Laban. The two had different gods of their fathers, yet they took an oath and agreed in the name of their own god to protect their agreement. They created a pillar between them to represent a witness and they agreed that their own gods would keep watch *between* them. Then, following ancient custom, they made a sacrifice and joined together in a meal of confirmation. Critical in this covenant was the warning that (in my words) *"my god is watching you, so be careful that you don't do something bad to our family and harm them."* Some have misinterpreted this as a sweet covenant asking God to watch over, protect and bless the other. *Indeed this covenant was a warning.*

Jacob was now standing confidently and ready for his family's independence. He was now freed from the deceit of this father-in-law. It had been a long time in coming. He had been working for his father-in-law for twenty years and it had been hard, grueling work, with a change in wages over ten times. After Laban kissed and blessed his family, they both went their own way.

Now Jacob followed his own God, who was sending him back to the land of his birth, the land given to Abraham and Isaac. Jacob was on his way to continue the Abrahamic Covenant. *He was going home.*

PRAYER: Dear God, you are with us through struggles, heartache, and tough times. You know the outcome. I trust in you and commit to your will in all things. Amen

NOTES:

PREPARATION
AND FEAR

SCRIPTURE: Genesis 32: 1- 21
KEY VERSE: Genesis: 32: 11

Have you ever been really afraid that you and your family would be harmed? Friends of ours had a house fire that caused that type of fear. Other neighbors who had their home broken into in the middle of the night had that type of fear. My Dad tells the story of the fear he had in World War II, for himself and his army of soldiers as they prepared to take over a Nazi occupied barn and house. He said he prayed really hard the night before the successful withdrawal and afterwards thanked God for their protection. My Dad's dedication and leadership resulted in receiving a bronze star.

Jacob feared for his life. His brother, Esau, was

coming to meet him after twenty years of being separated. Jacob had hurt his brother, stolen his father Isaac's blessing, and left town, knowing Esau wanted to murder him. Jacob was also afraid for his family. He sent messengers ahead to Esau to arrange a meeting and to scope things out. The messenger's return warning was that Esau was coming with 400 men. Assuming Esau was planning a revenge attack, Jacob, in distress, made plans. First, he planned to separate his family, servants, and livestock into two divisions, so one could flee as the other was being attacked. His second strategy was to send great gifts ahead of his meeting with Esau, so his brother would receive him graciously. Perhaps these strategies were built on the guilt of what he had previously done to Esau.

Jacob did not want a struggle with Esau. He had just finished a twenty-year conflict with Laban and wanted peace. He knew he needed the protection of the God of Abraham and Isaac. Jacob thought he was prepared. He prayed to God for safety the night before the meeting with his twin. But he was not prepared for what was to happen to him that same night in his own camp. It would be an unexpected and memorable struggle for life.

PRAYER: Almighty God, when I am afraid, I will trust in you . I put my faith in you alone to save me from harm and to guide my life. Amen.

NOTES

WRESTLING A
NEW NAME

SCRIPTURE: *Genesis 32:22-32*
KEY VERSE: *Genesis 32: 28*

Have you had an unforgettable encounter with God? Some describe hearing the voice of the Holy Spirit in their minds while praying. Others recall divine encounters in their dreams, or they are awakened in the early morning hours feeling the presence of the Holy Spirit. Jacob had his own unforgettable encounters. Remember his amazing dream of the stairway to heaven where Jacob sensed God's presence? And now another encounter! This story of Jacob's wrestling match with the Almighty had to have been the pinnacle of all of Jacob's spiritual encounters. We don't know if it was truly physical or spiritual. According to the scripture, Jacob wrestled all night with God and when it was over, he had a new name, *Israel*. He was forever changed.

The stories in Genesis show God at work intimately with His chosen ones. God spoke to Adam and Eve in the Garden of Eden. God told Noah to get prepared for a flood and to build an ark and even gave him the plans. God called Abram to leave his home in Haran and become the father of many nations. God told Hagar that Ishmael would become the father of twelve tribes. God gave Sarai a new name and promised her a son. God appeared to Isaac at Beersheba where he built an altar and heard God's spoken promise of protection, provision, and prosperity. God told Rebekah to expect twins and described how the older would serve the younger. Now a new Jacob, *renamed Israel* would continue the legacy of God's covenant and the Almighty would walk with him.

God desired an intimate relationship with his ancient people. They were specially chosen to carry out the magnificent plan that would ultimately lead to the Messiah through the line of King David. I believe God still has that desire for an intimate relationship with us today. His plans for us in this world of ours are always in motion. May we hear God's voice!

PRAYER: Almighty God, thank you for drawing close to us. Your plans for the world are more than we can ever begin to imagine. Speak to my heart, Lord. Make your presence known. Amen

NOTES:

BROTHERLY LOVE

SCRIPTURE: Genesis 33

KEY SCRIPTURE: Genesis 33: 4

When we have had conflict in the past with someone and haven't seen them in a long time, we speculate how difficult reuniting will be. Twenty years was a long time for Jacob and Esau to be apart, especially after the deception of the stolen blessing. Jacob was worried, cautious and afraid. Stiff and nervous Jacob was pushing gifts on Esau to show respect. Jacob desperately needed forgiveness. Esau was loving, openly affectionate, referring to Jacob as brother. When Esau accepted Jacob's gifts, Jacob became aware of Esau's forgiveness and expressed his happiness.

Esau, excited to reunite, offered to accompany Jacob and family to his own home in Seir, expecting them to desire a visit. Jacob's response was lame, using his large family as an excuse for slowing down travel together. When Jacob offered to meet Esau in Seir at another time, Jacob knew he was never going to drop by. Old habits of deceit were hard for Jacob to break. Maybe he didn't care about spending time with Esau, or it would take too long and be too much trouble. Maybe he was just relieved and only wanted to find forgiveness, after all. Maybe Jacob had places to go and people to see.

Jacob had experienced the highs of divine revelation and a new spiritual name. He had suffered the highs and lows of conflict with Laban and the sweet revelation of Esau's forgiveness. He had been blessed by wives and children. He was ready to be God's leader of the covenant for the remainder of his life.

We, too, can accept God's request for our leadership role today. We can be one of many who take the loving and peaceful call of God into the world. May we do that together!

PRAYER: Dear God, thank you for the family and friends you have placed in my life. Teach me to be loving and respectful of those relationships. May my friendships mirror your Godly characteristics. Amen

NOTES:

THE RAPE OF DINAH

Scripture: Genesis 34
Key Verse: Genesis 34: 2-6

Getting situated in a new town takes time and effort, especially when you buy land, build a home, and meet the neighbors. Jacob actively involved himself in the pagan city of Shechem in Canaan. He bought a lot from the sons of Hamor the Hivite, the founding father of Shechem. He wanted to meet the residents! Discover the city! Unfortunately, it wasn't a great start.

Jacob heard through the town's grapevine that Hamor's son, Shechem, had defiled his daughter, Dinah. Shechem apparently had eyes for her, and his sexual desires took over his common sense. It was love at first sight as he spotted her gadding about town. He asked his father to arrange their union. Shechem's father, Hamor, met with Jacob to discuss how intermarrying would help the families. Hamor invited Jacob's tribe to settle among them and offered a bride price that would include wealth, trade, and land ownership.

Jacob's sons were upset and angry. They decided to avenge the disgrace on their sister Dinah. Pretending to support the marriage they demanded the circumcision of all the town's males. Surprisingly, all the town's men agreed. Three days later, while the males were still healing, Dinah's brothers, Simeon and Levi, thoroughly plundered the city, and killed every male. Jacob angrily forecast much wrath to come from the Canaanites and other locals. He demanded justification from his two sons. The answer from Dinah's brothers was that (my words): *our sister should never have been treated like a prostitute.* The story highlights the differences between people and their beliefs; and how heated anger and conflict can be destructive. In future Genesis stories we will discover that the Almighty held these two brothers to account for their sin.

We really don't always know what our role will be when we are involved in conflict situations, whether in a church, business, school, society, personal or family relationship. God calls us to be levelheaded and act in a Godly way. It is sometimes difficult to hold our passion at bay. When we pray and identify what role God desires that we have, we can be assured we will not be alone. God is always with us.

PRAYER: Dear God, help us to navigate our relationships. May we be wise in choosing friendships and love relationships that are the best for us. Amen

NOTES:

THE CALL TO BETHEL

SCRIPTURE: *Genesis 35: 1-15*

KEY VERSES: *Genesis 35:1*

I remember my dear father calling me home. My mother was dying, and the family was gathering. I didn't hesitate. Maybe you have had a "come home call " for a variety of reasons, prompting your immediate return. Perhaps it is when you have heard God's call to ministry. Mine was a beautiful, sweet call that I could not ignore. I knew for certain what path I needed to take.

Jacob returned to Bethel at *God's invitation.* He could not ignore the call. It was the place where he first talked with God, the one who had been with him since the beginning. He remembered his first steps in the divine chosen path. Jacob continued his obedience. With the call to Bethel, he obeyed. *Like Abraham, Jacob listened to God's call and obeyed.*

So far in our Genesis stories, the Patriarchs were obedient to God's many requests. Their obedience must surely have been a beautiful sign of love toward God. With each action of obedience, God blessed them and repeated his covenant. God blessed Jacob, repeated the Abrahamic Covenant, gave Jacob the new name Israel, and provided blessings that he and his offspring would receive. Jacob was the third chosen one to receive God's covenant. God called each Patriarch to a divine path, and they matured in their call as their path became clearer.

Sometimes it is not easy to define our divine life path. Whether a choice of career, marriage partner, place to live or handling circumstances, we have a divine path. When we identify God's call how do we respond? Like Abraham do we get up and GO? Do we question the call? Do we delay the call?

I believe that God's specialty is *highlighting new paths.* In God's divine way, we see our path becoming clearer. When God shines his divine flashlight on us, we eventually see when, where and why we should respond. It just takes time, prayer, and awareness.

PRAYER: Heavenly Father, thank you for your divine path in our lives. Sometimes it feels like I need a flashlight in the darkness. Then you shine your divine light, and it becomes clearer. Thank you for walking with me and loving me. You have been with me wherever I have gone. Amen

NOTES:

BIRTH, LIFE AND DEATH

SCRIPTURE: Genesis 35:16-29
KEY VERSES: Genesis 35: 19

The truth is we are born, live, and die. Today when we remember people's lives, we describe our love for them, our memories and the legacy they left behind. If we were speaking at a memorial service about the Patriarchs, what would we mention and what story would we tell?

Sometimes we can read between the lines of scripture to feel the emotions of the characters in the story. Rachel died in childbirth when Jacob was taking his family to his home. Surely, he wanted old friends and family to see her. We know she was loved by Jacob whose heart was saddened by her death. What words did Rachel say before dying after the difficult birth of Benjamin? What did Jacob think about when he prepared Rachel's pillar at her burial spot on the road to Bethlehem? Did he hope one day to bury her in the family tomb? Was Rachel ever really happy and what was she thinking when she stole her father's idols?

Did Rachel and Leah ever truly make amends? Did Rachel continue to think she was a failure because having babies was difficult? How did Jacob deal with the loss of the love of his life, while answering God's call and stepping up as the Patriarch? Scripture is silent. We can only imagine.

When Jacob finally arrived home in Mamre, he was with his father, Isaac, who lived to be one hundred and eighty years old. Jacob and Esau buried him in the family tomb in the cave of Machpelah. The scripture is silent on any more details other than his age, where he was buried and who was present at the burial.

When a family or friend passes, we long to know more about them. Maybe about their life, situations, feelings, loves, successes and failures. Sometimes, we can only piece together their experiences. I would treasure another moment to interview my deceased relatives. I have lots of questions to ask in Heaven.

Perhaps, today, you might ask your friend or family member for their stories, thoughts, feelings and aspirations. May God bless that conversation.

PRAYER: Dear God, help us to celebrate our ancestors by getting to know more about them and their lives. Thank you for being a God of wisdom, patience and forgiveness. Amen.

NOTES:

THE ACCOUNT
OF ESAU

SCRIPTURE: Genesis 36

KEY VERSE: Genesis 36:8

Once, at a family reunion, one of my brothers asked questions about lost and forgotten members in the extended family. What happened to them? Anyone heard? Where are they? Any contact info? *We are curious about our families.*

What about Esau? Genesis generally describes Esau as a rugged, prideful, rebellious, independent young male. His life was impacted by brother conflicts, parental favoritism, stolen birthright, and grudge plans to kill Jacob. Later, Esau settled in Seir (Edom), and became known as the Father of the Edomites (Genesis 36). He reconciled with Jacob, the two brothers resolved their differences and then came together to bury their father, Isaac (Genesis 35:29).

Scripture is generally silent about Esau's personal adult life. There are a few references about his activity and his personality. Influenced by anger toward his parents, Esau married many wives from Canaan. Esau's Hittite wives (Judith and two of Ishmael's daughters, Basemath and Mahalath), Hittite wife Adah and Hivite wife Oholibamah all were grief to his parents.

Thanks to scribes and record keeping, Genesis 36 gives us the best family legacy of Esau. It describes the great wealth of Esau's family, livestock and material goods creating his need for more space and land (thus the reason for his relocation to Seir from Canaan). There is a specific account of multiple wives, sons, and grandchildren, including their political importance in the land. Many family members were a succession of chiefs and kings. Today the descendants of Edom occupy the land between Southern Jordan and Israel. *Surely God had blessed Esau.*

Famous personalities often disappear into the landscape. Think of the actors, writers and politicians who were famous that we know very little about.

Stories in Genesis seem to be written mostly about the patriarchs and God's divine plan through them. Yet we still long to know more. We will never know the most intimate story of each individual. We can be thankful for the personalities that are revealed and be confident that we know all we really need to know for the lesson.

PRAYER: Dear God, you provided a lineage for Esau. Despite his prideful, rebellious nature you blessed him and gave him a future in your divine plan. Amen

NOTES:

JOSEPH

JOSEPH

SCRIPTURE: *Genesis 37: 1-18*

KEY VERSE: *Genesis 37:3-5*

It is normal for siblings to be jealous and fight among each other. I can recall many squabbles among my own children and as a child, with my own siblings. It's sometimes difficult for parents to be aware of their favoritism, and to treat all their children fairly. We have seen this situation in our patriarch stories. Joseph, son of Israel (Jacob) and Rachel is an interesting case study. He had stepbrothers, except for Benjamin, his only brother like him, born of Israel (Jacob) and Rachel.

Joseph felt special because his father, Israel, doted on him, showing favoritism. Because he was so much younger than his stepbrothers, Joseph received special attention from his aging father. Rachel,

Joseph's mother and Israel's favorite wife, died in childbirth with his brother Benjamin, the baby of the family. With just one aging parent remaining, Joseph had a lot of issues about his identity that prevented him from getting along with his brothers.

Joseph talked about his dreams, showing he was more special than his brothers. He dreamed of sheaves of grain all bowing down to his sheave. In another dream the sun, moon and eleven stars were bowing down before him. We do not know if the spirit of God sent those dreams or Joseph was full of himself. The situation was not going to get better because Joseph's descriptions of his dreams to his father and brothers created jealousy, and anger. And then there was that colorful coat that made Joseph feel superior!

Generally speaking, parents try to use strategies to help children get along with each other. It isn't easy, especially when a kid is having dreams that contribute to an incredible ego. Think it could be time for some family counseling? The Almighty had a different agenda.

PRAYER: Dear God, thank you for loving me and walking with me in my life. Help me to be less self-centered, yet confident in living. I put you first in all that I say and do. Amen

NOTES:

SOLD INTO SLAVERY

SCRIPTURE: Genesis 37:19-36
KEY VERSES: Genesis 37:19- 20

Have you ever been so sure of yourself and possibly naive that you moved ahead on a plan only to find that you had no support or camaraderie? It could likely be a time of disillusionment and disappointment to misjudge the support of your team or family. Joseph might have thought his brothers would be proud of him and support him in his grand future. When he told them about his dreams, their response was probably not what he expected. They were sick and tired of his youthful ego and jealous that he was their father's favorite. And his dreams and that fancy coat of many colors were the last straw!!

When his father Israel sent him to check on his brothers in the field, he apparently had no idea that they hated him so. These brothers wanted to kill their brat of a brother who overestimated his own glory. The result was a mean-spirited case of ridding themselves of their brother, fooling their father that Joseph had been killed, and selling Joseph into slavery to Ishmaelites who in turn sold him to Potiphar, Pharaoh's official in Egypt. When told that Joseph was killed by a ferocious animal, Israel was beside himself and mourned.

It is so easy to see this story as a case of out-of-control brothers who treat their stepbrother beyond the bounds of decency. Could it be a lesson for Joseph about hubris? Sometimes stuff happens to us that seems at the time to be horrible. But later we realize that it was part of God's plan to prepare and equip us to serve Him. Joseph needed comeuppance and apparently his father, Israel, wasn't interested or equipped to provide that discipline.

We don't always recognize the divine plan until later. Joseph would survive his mistreatment and learn from it. Later, he would thank God for His grace and blessings. We can learn from his lesson that patience and humility are valued characteristics.

PRAYER: Thank you, God, for the tough times that we face that make us stronger, resilient, and prepared for adversity. Your plan is a mystery. May we trust in you. Amen

NOTES

JUDAH AND TAMAR

SCRIPTURE: *Genesis 38*

KEY VERSE: *Genesis 38:25-26*

As a young girl, I enjoyed Halloween because I could dress up like someone else. I could become a witch, princess, or a ghost. No one would know I was just the Wooten girl down the street. And I relished it! In this Genesis 38 story, Tamar, a widow, disguises herself as a shrine prostitute to deceive Judah, son of Jacob.

Tamar was the daughter- in -law of Judah. Since her husband's death, she'd been waiting for her brother-in-law, Onan, to fulfill his duty to impregnate her in the name of his deceased brother. Onan died without success, and Tamar waited for a younger brother, Shelah, to fulfill that role. Time was ticking and Tamar desperately wanted a child from the family line. Judah was delaying offering his third son. Knowing Judah's wife had died, Tamar hatched a plan. Judah was traveling to Timnah, so Tamar dressed as a shrine prostitute, and sat along the road hoping to capture his attention. The costume fooled Judah, who did not recognize her. After their "encounter," Tamar requested a gift to hold Judah responsible to pay her. Judah's seal, a cord, and staff were the gift of promise. Three months later, a pregnant Tamar claimed her due from Judah, by showing his seal, cord and staff. A repentant Judah declared her righteous.

Tamar gave birth to twins. Perez was her firstborn, who later became the leader of Judah's clan, the ancestor of David and the Messiah! Why is this story in the middle of Joseph's story? Perhaps the scribes saw it as another example of God's divine work and wanted to include it to remind us. Surely, God works in mysterious ways. Think about it! A woman disguised as a prostitute becomes the mother of the line of David. It is an incredible story with a divine ending! Who would have ever believed it. But it is true! See how Almighty God works!! Nothing is impossible or improbable with God! Ponder and pray what that means for you.

PRAYER: Almighty One: We see how you work and the wonders of your blessings! Just when we are down and out, we see what you do to transform and bless us! Thank you, Lord. Amen

NOTES:

JOSEPH AND POTIPHAR'S WIFE

SCRIPTURE: Genesis 39
KEY VERSE: Genesis 39: 20-21

Ever accused of something you didn't do? Years ago, my two youngest children were eyeing the chocolate chip cookies I had just baked. As I temporarily left the kitchen, I asked them not to eat them since they were hot. I was surprised to see chocolate mouths when I returned. When I asked "Why?" the youngest spoke up. "He ate one and gave me one, so I ate it!" Sound familiar? After discussion, I realized she had "kinda" falsely accused her brother. He had given one to his sister first, then saying "why not?" took one for himself. Details! I reminded them of the story of how God tossed the first couple out of Eden for disobeying and eating the forbidden fruit. Probably not a good example. My son asked, "Mom, are you going to throw us out of our house because we ate a cookie? I just had to laugh out loud.

Being falsely accused of making advances toward Potiphar's wife was not a funny story for Joseph. Potiphar was one of Pharaoh's officials as captain of the guard. His wife had eyes on handsome Joseph and asked him repeatedly to go to bed with her. Joseph's reply was always "no." Upset at his answer, she lied to her husband that Joseph had attempted to pressure her for sex. That's how Joseph landed in prison, but God protected him.

The LORD stayed with Joseph and took care of him. Joseph must have learned an important lesson because of Potiphar's wife's deception. Be careful of the situation you find yourself in. Always stay guarded. But his greatest lesson was witnessing God's care and protection while in prison. Joseph would mature in prison and learn many lessons.

Maybe you are in a terrible position at home or at work. You wonder when or how you could leave and land somewhere better. Maybe it's taking longer than you expected and you are frustrated. Pray for guidance and observe what lesson you are learning about God care.

PRAYER: Dear God, I see how you protected Joseph. Thank you for your protection and love for me. Amen.

NOTES:

DREAMS OF THE CUPBEARER AND THE BAKER

SCRIPTURE: Genesis 40: 1-23

KEY VERSE: Genesis 40:14

Do you believe your dreams have meaning ? Some people dream of flying above the trees. Others describe dreams of going to work or class in their birthday suit! Could these be dreams of power or vulnerability? Recall that as a young boy, Joseph had symbolic dreams that angered his brothers and caused distress. Later in life an older Joseph had symbolic dreams, and God gave him the gift for interpreting them—his own and others.

In Genesis 40, we observe Joseph interpreting the dreams of two of Pharaoh's servants, the Chief

Cupbearer, and Chief Baker. Having the title "Chief" before your occupation meant that you were the "boss", and Pharaoh trusted you. You never wanted to upset his highness. These two individuals apparently offended Pharaoh for something they had done and were thrown in prison, alongside Joseph. When Joseph met them, they were afraid because they needed help to interpret the symbolism in their own dreams. They needed help getting out of their prison situation. Joseph offered his interpretation that the Cupbearer would be restored to his position, and the Baker would be hanged. Both interpretations came true. Afterwards, Joseph reminded the Cupbearer to tell the Pharaoh of his unique gift of dream interpretation just in case the Pharaoh needed help. Unfortunately for Joseph, the Baker forgot him. Joseph remained in prison for two more years. Finally, the Cupbearer remembered him when the Pharaoh needed help to interpret his own dreams. It was never too late to help. It was just enough time for Joseph to mature and grow as a faithful, young man!

There's a lesson here for us. Sometimes, we are unhappy when we don't get what we think we deserve. We think that God is abandoning or punishing us.

The Almighty works on a different schedule. His time frame is often not ours. God always has a perfect plan.

PRAYER: *Dear God, teach me patience and understanding as you discipline me and prepare me for your will. Help me see your goodness in all things. Amen.*

NOTES:

PHARAOH'S DREAM

SCRIPTURE: Genesis 41
KEY VERSE: Genesis 41:15-16

Sometimes, you have to wait for positive things to happen. You try to hang in there hoping for good results. Maybe you even forget all about it, then "out of the blue" your prayers are answered. A friend of mine married a young man that her parents didn't like. There was much tension affecting their relationship with the couple. Years later as the parents saw what a great man, husband, and father he had become, they confessed how happy they were that he had married their daughter. They truly loved him and were so proud of him! God is uniquely at work in our lives changing our attitudes, and our opinions, and teaching us to love.

Joseph could have languished in prison waiting

to be free. However he instead spent much time maturing and growing in his faith in God. He was such a boy" full of himself" when he was captured, sold and brought to Egypt. God was preparing Joseph for his future. When the time was right, Pharaoh called Joseph to interpret his dreams because the Chief Cupbearer remembered him. Joseph was successful in interpreting his dreams and offering suggestions to handle the coming famine. His suggestions prepared Pharaoh to plan for seven years of growing and storing grain and then during the famine to have enough supply on hand to feed the people.

Pharaoh trusted this now thirty-year-old Joseph and placed him in charge of his Palace and the entire land of Egypt. Joseph gave the credit for his talents and wisdom to his God. He had grown into the Godly man that Pharaoh admired. God blessed all that Joseph did, giving him a wife and two sons, as well as great leadership role in Egypt. God was at work in all of Joseph's life. And God had even more surprises in store!

Maybe unaware of how God is working in your life, you feel stuck in a relationship or in a career. You know you would like a change but are unsure where to turn. Patience, prayer and trust in God is a great place to begin. God most likely has surprises in store for you.

PRAYER: Dear God, how amazing you are! Your plans for us are more than we ever could imagine! Your blessings are more than we deserve. Thank you for loving and teaching us how to live for you. Amen

NOTES:

BROTHERS IN EGYPT

SCRIPTURE: Genesis 42

KEY VERSE: Genesis 42:8

How does it feel to see relatives or friends you haven't seen in years? Perhaps you don't even recognize them, especially if they were children or teenagers when you last saw them. I recently sent out a Christmas card picture of our large family of children and grandchildren. Many of our friends and relatives living far away had not seen them for years! The most frequently made comment was that they didn't even recognize them because they were so grown up! When Joseph's brothers saw him in Egypt after twenty years, they didn't recognize him as he had become an adult.

Famine now was severe in all the land and countries came to Egypt to buy grain that had been stored during good times. Joseph's brothers were among those shoppers. Joseph, now much older and governor of the land of Egypt, was selling the grain, and recognized his brothers, but pretended he did not. The brothers didn't recognize him. Joseph harshly accused his brothers of being spies, took brother Simeon hostage, and used this tactic to get them to return with their young brother, Benjamin. Then, unknown to the brothers, Joseph gave orders for the silver they paid for their purchase to be returned in their sacks of grain. Surely, Jacob must have schemed that would put fear in their hearts and create their need to return with the money and beg for leniency.

Joseph's choices of dealing with his brothers seem manipulative, and dramatic. Why did Joseph create these strategies in order to see his brothers again? Why the harsh tactics? Getting even for what they had done to him? Why wasn't Joseph honest? Too much too soon? Need more thinking time? God's plan all along? Was Joseph relying on God or his dreams for decisions? Joseph's complicated story continues.

Do we, ourselves, sometimes turn simple solutions in our lives into dramatic, complicated and manipulative strategies? We can be better than that. Let's turn to God.

PRAYER: Dear God, thank you for our families and for your plans for our lives. Thank you for "coincidences" that are part of your plan. Help us see the best way to handle issues within our relationships. May your love permeate our decisions and flow into our family relationships. Amen

NOTES:

RETURN TO EGYPT

SCRIPTURE: Genesis 43
KEY LESSON: Genesis 43:15

It is my joy to take gifts to family when going for a visit. Candy, cash, toys and books are popular with grandchildren as are unique gifts for their parents. It is also fun to treat them to a favorite restaurant to celebrate birthdays or just hang out with each other. Celebrating with family is always a good thing!

Jacob (Israel) sent gifts with his sons when they returned to Egypt to buy more grain and to bring their youngest brother, Benjamin, to meet Joseph. The brothers and their father Jacob were nervous about how they might be received by Joseph. They hoped that the gifts would appease this difficult, angry Egyptian governor.

When they arrived, a great feast had been prepared

for them in Joseph's home. The atmosphere was celebratory as they ate and drank heartily. Benjamin was treated in a special way and the hostage brother, Simeon, was returned to his family. Joseph, still unrecognized by his brothers, was sensitive and emotional, weeping in private after seeing Benjamin and enjoying his brothers. We might wonder what will happen next. When will Joseph reveal himself to his brothers? Is this dinner celebration too good to be true?

Maybe you have been with family in a conflict situation and been uncomfortable wondering when something terrible might resurface. You hope and pray that the celebration continues, and family members reunite. Perhaps you have an idea of what Joseph's brothers might think or feel. Are they confused, relieved, questioning and wondering about the outcome? For Joseph and his family there is hope as the *story continues.*

For us, our God desires that our families love one another, and His Spirit is at work individually, and in entirety when we are together. This story is a wonderful lesson about how God views the importance of families. We are an important element in God's creation plan. And we are better united than apart.

PRAYER: Dear Lord, you know the outcome in our lives. You orchestrated this moment in time with Joseph and his brothers. You are the one who brings us together when we have broken apart as a family. May we listen to you. Hold us close and show us the way. Amen

NOTES:

THE SILVER CUP

SCRIPTURE: Genesis 44

KEY VERSES: Genesis 44:33-34

I cherish the gifts and cards my children received at their birth. Along with their baby shoes and special baby blanket, their silver spoon and baby cup were stored in a box and given to my children when they were adults. Those items remind us of their arrival into the world.

Joseph had a silver cup that was important to him, marking his significance, role, and status in Pharoah's kingdom. He also used it for divination to predict the future and interpret dreams. Joseph used this silver cup to design a fake theft, hiding it in Benjamin's grain sack to hold his little brother responsible. When Benjamin was accused of theft, it caused all the brothers to return to Egypt. Their fear was that

Benjamin would be held to account and become Joseph's slave.

In a most poignant moment, Judah offers to take the place of Benjamin as a slave, so that his little brother can return to his father, Jacob (Israel.) He becomes a substitute for Benjamin and his "sin of thievery." Perhaps this offer to take Benjamin's place is foreshadowing Jesus's sacrifice on the cross as a substitute for us and our sins? Is this a glimpse again of the importance of the genealogical line of Judah to King David, and thus to the Messiah?

It is easy to grow weary of all of Joseph's shenanigans. Is he dragging his feet to reveal himself? Can we forgive his fake theft strategy because he wants to spend more time with Benjamin, his biological brother? Is this a writer's technique to build emotion in the story plot of Joseph's interaction with his brothers. It is time for answers and solutions.

Perhaps this dramatic story of Joseph and his brothers is like your life. Maybe you have friends and family who need to provide answers and solutions about their interactions with you and each other. You may want all this drama in your life to stop. If so, take it to God in prayer. The Almighty has answers and ways to solve each and every problem. And remember God specializes in conflict issues!

PRAYER: Almighty God, you are the all-knowing. Your plans and designs are perfect. You can take our feeble actions and use them for good. Thank you for your patience and love. Amen

NOTES:

GOD SENT ME AHEAD

SCRIPTURE: *Genesis 45*

KEY VERSE: *Genesis 45: 5*

Have you ever thought that you were in the right place at the right time? Maybe you were hired in a job because you had experience you had accumulated over many years. Or maybe you met your spouse to be while you were on a trip you took randomly. You thought it was an unbelievable coincidence, but it worked out beautifully. Was it <u>God's plan,</u> orchestrated all along? Think about it!?

Joseph, at thirty-nine, gave God the credit for his arrival in Egypt and also "randomly" meeting his long-lost stepbrothers and younger brother. Joseph believed that God had sent him to Egypt ahead of time to save his families' lives during the famine. When Joseph revealed to his brothers who he really was, he was emotional and wept. Terrified about the situation, the brothers were unsure how to behave. Joseph assured them, invited them to come to Egypt to live in Goshen and offered them a new life. The entire family was invited by Pharaoh to come receive land, jobs, supplies, clothing, animals, and grain. Picture this scene of weeping, hugging, kissing, laughing, and jumping up and down. Plenty of forgiveness from Joseph and the power of God for all of them! When Israel (Jacob) was updated on the news, he thanked God that Joseph was alive and well.

Have you ever been so excited about God's grace and blessings upon you? Family love, forgiveness and grace are powerful things to experience. Upon receiving such an abundance of God's love, I have wept and jumped for joy, thanking God, who loves our joy as we receive His will! God is so good!!

PRAYER: Heavenly Father, thank you for your blessings and the beauty of your plan for us. My love for you overflows and joy fills my heart. Amen

NOTES:

JACOB IN EGYPT

SCRIPTURE: Genesis 46-47

KEY VERSE: Genesis 46a: 3-4

Have you ever had a really big move? One of our moves was so large that when the truck was filled, the movers still had items remaining on the driveway. We had to load up our family van and then donate the leftovers. *Maybe we just had too much stuff?* Moving is hard work, especially when you are going to another city or nation. You have to find a job if you don't have one, so what will you do?

Joseph had the answer for all these issues when he moved his entire Caanan family to Goshen (the district of Rameses) in Egypt. Ever the salesman, Joseph coached his brothers to speak freely about their occupation, so that they could settle in Goshen as the expert shepherds that they were. Pharaoh gave them the land they needed for their livestock and offered to hire experts among the family to be in charge of his own livestock. Pharaoh was generous to Joseph and his family and settled them in the best part of Goshen. The Israelites, as they were known, grew in number and acquired much land and assets.

In the meantime, during the continued famine, Joseph negotiated with people to pay for their grain with their livestock and land. He devised a law where they could work the land and keep the grain but return one-fifth of the product to the Pharaoh.

Joseph's God-given leadership ability created a good environment for the people of Egypt. Just as God blessed Joseph, God blesses us with talents and abilities. When we are successful in life, we can give God the credit for His abundant grace and the outpouring of His love.

When you evaluate your life and the paths that God has led you down, it is not difficult to see that the negative moments taught you and changed you. The positive moments resulted from lessons learned from a God who loves you immensely. Without lessons, we would become stagnant and weak. We can thank God for those blessings.

PRAYER: Heavenly Father, thank you for your blessings and the gifts of opportunities that you provide in our life. The talents and gifts we possess are from you. Amen

NOTES:

BLESSINGS ON MANASSEH AND EPHRAIM

SCRIPTURE: Genesis 48
KEY VERSE: Genesis 48: 18-19

Have you ever received a special "family heirloom gift" from a parent or a relative? Maybe it was a ring or bracelet, or a car, furniture, or tool. These highly valued items were passed down from generation to generation, and perhaps were considered a special blessing by the previous owner. Blessing a child or a young adult in ancient times was considered an act of love and fatherly responsibility. Generally speaking, the legal and societal expectation was that the blessing went along with the inheritance given to the eldest son.

Despite ancient expectations, in Genesis we have seen favoritism toward the second son, such as with Jacob chosen over Esau and Isaac chosen over Ishmael. In Genesis 48 we find Jacob's blessings also given to Joseph's younger son, Ephraim. How did this choice of younger son transpire? Knowing his father was near death, Joseph, as was custom, took his two sons to receive their grandfather Jacob's blessing. It must have been an emotional time, especially when Jacob surprisingly chose his younger grandson Ephraim to receive God's blessing of Abraham and Isaac. Jacob spoke what he believed to be God's choice for the ancestral line. However, when Joseph attempted to correct his father's choice, Jacob stated firmly that Manasseh would become great, yet his younger brother Ephraim would become greater. Grandfather Jacob would now legally adopt his grandsons as his own, and split Joseph's share of inheritance fifty-fifty with them. Therefore, Joseph would become the father of two tribes in his sons' names. God made his choices known for His people, the Jews. *Ephraim and Manasseh would become known as the House of Israel.*

As parents and grandparent we can bless our families and bequeath the spiritual and physical resources for them to use as they grow into the family leadership role. Telling our children and grandchildren how much God loves them, and how proud we are of them sends a message of love. It is our blessing over them.

PRAYER: Dear God, thank you for our families. We remember and honor those who came before us; and bless and support those who come after us. Thank you for your plans for Israel, and for creating the ancestral line of Abraham, Isaac, and Jacob, which led to the line of the Messiah. Amen.

NOTES:

JACOB BLESSES
HIS SONS

SCRIPTURE: Genesis 49
KEY VERSE: Genesis 49: 1

It is never easy to have experienced the passing of a family member. If time permits, the loved one may want to gather with the family to say final words or a blessing. The family may then recall the life of the departed with heartwarming and sometimes funny stories. *It is all about being family!*

There's a record of Jacob's final words to his sons in Genesis 49: 1-28. It is referred to as *"the Blessing of Jacob."* Jacob (Israel) describes the future for his sons who become known as the Twelve Tribes of Israel. This poem is the grand finale in Genesis of God's plans to call Abraham to receive the gift of the land and the blessings God has for their offspring. That promise has been fulfilled through Abraham, Isaac, Jacob, and Joseph. Israel's predictions for the future come from a wise father who understands the power of God's plans. He gives blessings appropriate to each one of his sons.

Those who have disobeyed God such as **Reuben**'s sexual acts, or the violence of **Simeon and Levi** will have life consequences. **Judah** is praised and rewarded with the line of David (the scepter). **Zebulun** will prosper from the sea, **Issachar** will work hard, **Dan** will provide justice for his people, **Gad** will be protector of his people, **Asher**'s rich food will provide delicacies, **Naphtali** will be a free spirit, **Joseph** will be a fruitful vine of great blessings, and **Benjamin's** exploits will be like the wolf, ravaging and plundering.

Israel's last request was to be buried in the cave near Mamre in Canaan, the burial place of Abraham and Sarah, Isaac and Rebekah, and Leah. There he would rest in peace with God.

PRAYER: Dear God, your plans for Abraham, Isaac, Jacob, and Joseph are fulfilled. Your plans continue through all generations to follow. Thank you for accomplishing your will through our faith in you. Amen

NOTES:

A LETTER ON FORGIVENESS

SCRIPTURE: Genesis 50
KEY VERSES: Genesis 50:16-17

Ever find a letter that someone who had died had left behind for you to read? My husband and his sister found a sealed envelope left behind by their mother marked: *"Read after I am gone."* After opening it they began to laugh. It was a solution to sharing an heirloom valued by the entire family. Always avoiding conflict, Mother J was unable to decide which person was entitled to receive the item. Mother J suggested they alternate every other year to enjoy the item and added that they meet for lunch to do the hand off. They could visit, keep in touch, and share the item. And to this day, they follow those instructions. Aren't families great???

Well, it appears that a left behind letter from Jacob (Israel) was meant to solve a problem of forgiveness. It was a letter of instructions to Joseph's brothers to apologize for the incredibly mean act they committed against Joseph when he was just a teenager. They had intended to kill him out of jealousy but ended up selling him into slavery. Now that Jacob had died, would Joseph then get even? This was no laughing matter! Joseph forgave them immediately, while realizing God was in the plan all along. Even though the brothers meant it for harm, God used it for good to place Joseph where he could help Egypt and save so many hurting lives. He assured his brothers not to be afraid, that he would continue to provide for them.

God's plan triumphs as Genesis comes to an end. On his deathbed, at the old age of one hundred and ten years, Joseph reminded his family that God had given an oath to Abraham, Issac, and Jacob to return them to the land he had given them. Joseph asked that they take his bones back there when they return. *That return to the Promised Land does occur and is recorded in the Book of Exodus, as God's covenant with his people continues.*

PRAYER: Almighty One, thank you for your promise to continue the plan you gave to Abraham, Issac, and Jacob. Your promises and plans never fail. Thank you for protecting, saving and loving us. Amen

NOTES:

AUTHOR'S NOTES
ON THE EVENTS
IN GENESIS

AUTHOR'S NOTES ON THE EVENTS IN GENESIS

You have finished the Genesis stories. Sometimes the stories were sad and tedious, yet many were incredible, joyful, and amazing. You have experienced the Patriarchs up close in a beautifully written story of their lives, walking with their LORD GOD.

The Genesis story tells us God's divine plan for them and how they responded to the call. We also get a glimpse of their character and issues in their lives. They and their family members are presented as often flawed, imperfect, manipulative, jealous, deceitful and egocentric. However, throughout the stories, we begin to realize how God was shaping and preparing the Patriarchs and family members in a powerful way. God was at work and present in their lives. That makes Genesis an important story.

You have read in the pages of Genesis about the human condition (sin), and God's grace, faithfulness, blessings and trustworthiness. In every one of these stories, God's all-knowing plan has prevailed. Those who sinned greatly were punished. Those who were faithful were often given tasks and difficult lives yet were rewarded.

You have seen prophecy unfolding in stories containing the foreshadowing of the Messiah. You have read of human exploits that harmed others, and those that prepared the way for God's grace and God's almighty plans.

In Genesis we have our story. *It is us...you and me.* We are no different from those whose stories we have read. Some of us just take longer than others when it comes to being faithful.

My prayer is that you found yourself in these stories and have come to understand yourself better. *Our story* is not finished with Genesis. It continues next in Exodus and elaborates God's plan throughout the Hebrew Bible and the New Testament.

God's story is our story. And it isn't an easy one. We stumble, fall, fail, lash out, suffer, cry, blame and forgive, laugh and jump for joy! I end with some thoughts about Joseph and his story. I think they summarize all of the stories of Genesis.

Story of Joseph.

In Genesis 42, Joseph sees his brothers face to face after all they had been through such a long time ago. It set the stage for a long awaited, incredible family reunion. Joseph, despite his wisdom, take his sweet time to deal with revealing himself and showing love toward his family. It is agonizing as we observe the back and forth between the unidentified Joseph and the emotional roller coaster ride that he puts his brothers through. It is a long story in progress through the final chapter in Genesis 50. *This tedious story, read aloud, is meant to bother us,* as the listener swallows hard, awaiting the final ending. It is a balance against the long story of Joseph's pain and suffering, and his ordeal in Egypt and final success. God seems present, yet aloof sometimes. It seems to take forever. It unfolds the ways that Joseph unnecessarily makes life difficult for his brothers. Making them pay for what they had done to him? Getting even? Desire to see his younger brother, Benjamin, and Father Jacob? Pulling royal rank to frighten them? And finally, unveiling his identity leads to a long-awaited family reunion.

Joseph has all the characteristics of us: an ego of

superiority, desire to control the situation, and need for immediate gratification. Over time, God molds this young man into an incredible man of God. Joseph recognizes God's plan and extends forgiveness to his brothers.

While our own story may be different from the patriarchs, God is in the business of molding us and changing us so that we can participate in His plan. Each patriarch was led by God in a special way to fulfill the Almighty's mission and to establish the way for the Messiah. Each had a different personality and different gifts. In the end, they all were faithful and accomplished what God intended.

As we near the ending of this great family of God, the promise to the patriarchs continues to unfold and rests with Jacob's blessing of his family, who become The Twelve Tribes of Israel. Joseph reassures his brothers that God meant all of this for good, having brought the patriarchs to Egypt for such a time as this. The flight out of Egypt to the Promised Land is God's next step in fulfilling His covenant.

That is what we must pray for in our own lives. We pray to walk on the path God has planned for us, and that we are conformed and transformed in God's likeness despite our waywardness.

God bless you as you continue to place your life in the Potter's Hands.

Printed in the United States
by Baker & Taylor Publisher Services